MODERN **PRESSURE COOKER** BOOK

MODERN **PRESSURE COOKER** BOOK

GINA STEER

A QUINTET BOOK

Published by Apple Press
6 Blundell Street
London N7 9BH

ISBN 1 84092 311 3

This book was conceived, designed and produced by
Quintet Publishing Limited
6 Blundell Street
London N7 9BH

Senior Project Editor: Toria Leitch
Editor: Anna Bennett
Designer: Deep Design
Photographer: Ferguson Hill
Food Stylist: Vicki Smallwood

Creative Director: Richard Dewing

Typeset in Great Britain by Central Southern
Typesetters, Eastbourne
Manufactured in Hong Kong by Regent Publishing
Services Limited
Printed in China by Leefung-Asco Printers Trading
Limited

AUTHOR'S ACKNOWLEDGEMENTS

An enormous thanks to Juliet Barker, who has done a fantastic job in helping me test the recipes ensuring that
they all work well. Thanks also to Vicki Smallwood who has toiled so hard in a hot photographic studio to
produce such stunning pictures with photographer Ferguson Hill.

I would like to thank Prestige for their help while writing this book, and for the loan of pressure cookers for both
testing and photography of the recipes. Also to Divertimenti for the loan of a pressure cooker.

CONTENTS

INTRODUCTION

I have a vivid childhood memory of the steam and hissing coming from the pressure cooker as my mother cooked all manner of dishes and, of course, the inevitable occasional accident when our dinner, be it soup or casserole, ended up on the ceiling, much to my amusement and my mother's annoyance.

Time moves on, however, and pressure cookers are now state-of-the-art, stylish pieces of equipment, far safer and easier to use, and well suited to the twenty-first century lifestyle. Pressure cooking is healthy due to the minimal amount of fat used, which helps to reduce cholesterol levels. It is also quick. We are all living life on the edge with very little spare time and often find it difficult to cook a healthy, nutritious and delicious meal for our family and friends. A pressure cooker can provide such a meal in minutes so the pressure is on the pressure cooker rather than us.

If you are a newcomer to this method of cooking, I am confident that with a little practice you will not be able to imagine life without it. So welcome to the world of pressure cooking, which will give you twice the flavour in less than half the time.

PRESSURE COOKER BASICS

Before you start cooking with your pressure cooker there are a few imperative guidelines to bear in mind. There is a wide range of pressure cookers available and it is important that you read the manufacturer's instructions carefully before using yours for the first time because directions can vary from one model to another.

The principle behind pressure cooking is that ingredients and liquid are enclosed in the cooker, and the steam, which in a normal saucepan is allowed to escape freely, is controlled, thus increasing the pressure and cooking temperature. It is this high temperature as well as the steam being forced through the food that cooks the food quickly and tenderizes it at the same time. Under normal conditions water boils at 100°C/212°F; this is dictated by atmospheric pressure and cannot be increased however long the water boils. The cook control on the pressure cooker increases the pressure inside the cooker, which in turn raises the temperature at which the liquid boils, thus leading to the rapid cooking time.

With most cookers the prepared food is put into the cooker with the required amount of liquid. The amount of liquid is important because the pressure cooker must not boil dry while under pressure, so there should always be at least 300ml/½ pint in the cooker. The lid is then closed and fixed into position and the cooker placed over the heat and brought quickly to pressure. Then the heat is reduced slightly and the cooking time should then be timed.

GENERAL RULES FOR PRESSURE COOKING

- Never leave your pressure cooker unattended on a hot stove. This could result in the cooker boiling dry and will cause damage. If this should happen, switch off the heat and allow the cooker to cool before moving.

- Add sufficient liquid to the cooker. You will need at least 300 ml/$\frac{1}{2}$ pint of liquid to cover the first 15 minutes of cooking time then a further 150 ml/$\frac{1}{4}$ pint of liquid for every additional 15 minutes of cooking time.

- Never overfill your cooker and remember that different foods require different filling levels. With cereals, pulses, beans and lentils, for example, the cooker must be no more than one-third full including the liquid.

- With soups, rice, pasta and some stews the cooker should be no more than half-full including the liquid. Solid foods such as joints, vegetables and one-pot meals should be no more than two-thirds full.

- Ensure that your stove is suitable for your pressure cooker. The base of the pressure cooker should sit comfortably on the heat source and be of a similar size.

- If using gas make sure that the flames do not go up the sides of the pressure cooker.

- If using containers to cook inside the pressure cooker, make sure they are ovenproof and fit well. They need to be able to withstand a temperature of 130°C/262°F.

- Do not place containers on top of foods that swell during cooking such as rice, dried beans, cereals and pasta.

- When steaming, secure the greaseproof paper firmly. I have found that greaseproof paper is better than foil when steaming.

- Do not use metal or plastic in the cooker.

- Lightly oil the trivet when placing items of food on it to prevent sticking.

- If cooking dumplings, do not cook under pressure – otherwise the dumpling mixture may block the safety outlet on rising. Add the dumplings once the cooker has depressurized and do not close the lid.

- Finally, take care not to damage the various parts of the cooker because this will affect the efficiency of the cooker.

YOUR PRESSURE COOKER

When deciding what size of pressure cooker to buy, it is important that you consider your lifestyle. A 5-litre/9-pint cooker is sufficient as you become familiar with using a pressure cooker; a smaller cooker would be useful for cooking rices and grains while a larger cooker is ideal for stocks, or cooking in large quantities. Modern pressure cookers have back-up mechanisms, which prevent the build-up of excess pressure thus making the cookers far safer to use than earlier models. All will have the same features although these may be called by different names.

Modern cookers have a *rise and time indicator*. This is a small round plug that rises and indicates that the pressure cooker has reached and is maintaining the correct internal temperature. If it should fall down while cooking under pressure, most probably it is because the heat is too low on the base, so increase the heat slightly. The cookers also have a *ready to serve indicator* which is a rubber plug and pintle. This tells you what is happening inside the pressure cooker; the indicator rises when the cooker is sealed and drops down once the pressure has been released, thus allowing the lid to be released. Ensure at all times that the rise and time indicator and ready to serve indicator are kept clean and free from food particles. Clean gently with a soft brush and soapy water. Check the manufacturer's instructions.

Some cookers have two *cook controls*, some three, each a different weight. The weight that is used the most is the heaviest, 6.8 kg/15 lb, which works for most foods. The 4.5-kg/10-lb cook control is used for preserves and delicate foods and is often used for steaming puddings. When using the 4.5-kg/10-lb cook control, the rise and time indicator does not rise and the timing is carried out when there is a gentle hissing and escape of steam from around the weight.

If the heat setting is too high, a loud hissing will occur. Lower the base heat. If no hissing is heard, increase the base heat, as the setting is too low and the food will not cook.

If a 2.25-kg/5-lb cook control is provided this should be used for delicate foods as above.

Inside your cooker you will find a *separator*, which is a small basket ideal for cooking one-pot meals or small puddings or fish. If used for rice or pasta, line with foil. It is also useful for cooking different vegetables at the same time, as the separator can be sectioned with the dividers that sit inside the basket.

The *trivet* sits inside the cooker, rim-side down, often to place food on or to divide different types of food.

A rubber seal or *gasket* fits inside the lid and is vital to ensure that the cooker seals properly. It is important that the gasket is kept clean and it is a good idea to clean after each use and allow the gasket to dry naturally before refitting.

After cooking, remove the food as soon as possible from the cooker. Do not leave food in for long periods because this may cause staining. Wash in hot soapy water, rinse thoroughly and dry after each use. If any food sticks, either soak the cooker in soapy water for a short period or use a plastic scrubbing brush or steel wool. Do not use bleach because this will cause staining.

If any food has actually burnt on, make up a strong solution using cream of tartar and water, bring to the boil then simmer for about 20 minutes. Discard water and wash in soapy water, rinse and dry.

Add a little lemon juice to the water in the cooker when steaming to prevent discoloration.

If you use the cooker regularly, the gasket and ready to serve indicator will need to be changed about every 6 months.

TROUBLESHOOTING

- **Cooker will not come to pressure** – the ready to serve indicator or the lid gasket may be leaking. Lightly oil the gasket and if this does not work, replace the faulty part.

- **Lid gasket leaks** – the rim of cooker is dirty. Wash the gasket and cooker rim. If this does not work, check if the gasket is worn and replace if necessary. Check whether the body or lid of the cooker is damaged and if so return to manufacturer and ensure that the correct gasket is fitted.

- **Excess steam for cook control** – this could mean that the heat is too high, the weight is not fitted correctly or the weight support is loose. Either reduce the heat, or click the weight into place with a thick cloth or oven gloves and if the support is loose, cool the cooker, remove the weight and lid then tighten the weight support.

- **Ready to serve indicator and pintle rises and ejects steam vertically** – the weight support is blocked and cannot vent correctly. Cool then clean the cook control support and reset the ready to serve indicator.

- **Ready to serve indicator blows out completely** – the weight support is blocked. Cool, clean the cook control support and fit a new ready to serve indicator.

- **Cooker boils dry** – there are a couple of possible reasons: the lid gasket or the ready to serve indicator is leaking, in which case return to the manufacturer. This can also happen if you have been cooking on too high a heat for too long, or have used insufficient liquid for the cooking time.

TIPS AND TECHNIQUES

Cooking times vary with pressure cooking and times given can therefore only be a guide. When cooking vegetables, I have tried to undercook because it takes no time at all to return the cooker to pressure if necessary whereas once overcooked, vegetables cannot be recovered.

Ensure that the lid is locked firmly in place before you start to bring the cooker to pressure. Normally the lid will just slide and lock into the cooker. Many cookers have arrows or dots to indicate how to locate the lid. If the lid seems difficult to close, smear the inside of the rim of the lid with a little oil.

It can take from 30 seconds to 20 minutes to bring the food to pressure, depending on the food and quantity being cooked. To speed this time up use boiling, not cold, liquid.

Unless stated otherwise, the pressure cooking time commences once the pressure is reached. It is at this point that you should lower the heat and begin timing. If the pressure goes down, increase the heat slightly under the cooker as quickly as possible. It is important that the heat is lowered once pressure is reached: if not, the pressure will continue to rise, resulting in loud hissing sounds.

A heat diffuser is a good investment especially if your cooker is old. It also helps when cooking rice and dried beans, which may stick.

There are two ways of releasing the pressure: quickly (a method used for most foods) and depressurizing slowly (a method used for foods that may block up the vents such as rice, jam or milk puddings).

When using your cooker for steamed puddings it is important that a presteaming time is used. This is important to ensure that the rising agent will be able to work. Without this the puddings will be heavy and stodgy.

Check your manufacturer's handbook on how to presteam. Remember that these puddings are cooked under 4.5-kg/10-lb cook control and the rise and time indicator will not rise during the cooking process.

HINTS FOR COOKING
PASTA, RICE AND CEREALS

- Rice, pasta and cereals can be cooked in the base of the cooker as well as in the separator or a solid container. If cooking in the perforated separator, line with foil before cooking.

- Do not fill the cooker more than half-full and bring to pressure over a medium heat.

- Keep the heat slightly lower than usual to prevent the contents from frothing up and blocking any vents.

- Depressurize slowly.

- If using a container, ensure that it will fit inside the cooker then, if necessary, line with foil, place 225 g/8 oz pasta or rice into the container, pour in 450 ml/¾ pint boiling liquid then cover with greaseproof paper and secure.

- Use 6.8-kg/15-lb cook control unless otherwise stated and depressurize slowly after cooking.

- When cooking pearl barley or coarse oatmeal make sure that the cooker is not more than half-full and use 900 ml/1½ pints of boiling water for every 100 g/4 oz of grain. Bring to the boil over a medium heat and cook on a lower heat setting.

- Bulghur wheat and millet should be cooked in an ovenproof container or foil-lined separator, not in the body of the cooker. Depressurize slowly.

- Cooking rice with milk for puddings, only use 600 ml/1 pint milk to 50 g/2 oz rice. Bring the milk to the boil in the open cooker, add the rice and stir until it comes back to the boil. Lower the heat to a rolling boil, then close the lid and bring to 6.8-kg/15-lb pressure. Depressurize slowly.

COOKING TIMES

REMEMBER TO USE THE CORRECT AMOUNT OF LIQUID WHEN COOKING. THESE REQUIRE SLOW DEPRESSURIZING.

PASTA, RICE AND CEREALS

Variety	Cooking time
100 g/4 oz pearl barley	20 minutes
100 g/4 oz coarse oatmeal	15 minutes
225 g/8 oz long-grain rice	2 minutes
225 g/8 oz brown rice	3 minutes
225 g/8 oz spaghettini	2 minutes
225 g/8 oz spaghetti/tagliatelle	3 minutes

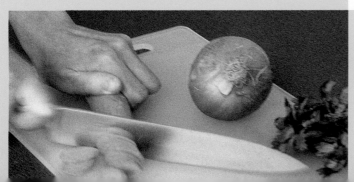

HINTS FOR COOKING **BEANS**

- With all dried beans it is very important to soak them in boiling water for at least 1 hour before cooking. Drain the beans and place in the cooker; do not fill the cooker more than one-third full after both the beans and liquid have been added.

- Add 600 ml/1 pint of fresh water or stock for every 225 g/8 oz of dried beans (this weight is before soaking).

- Do not add salt to the cooker when cooking beans as this toughens the beans. Season once the beans are done.

- Bring to the boil, remove any scum that floats to the surface, then reduce the heat so that the liquid is gently simmering before closing the lid. Bring to pressure at this simmering heat.

- Always depressurize slowly at the end of cooking time or the vents may become blocked.

- Use 6.8-kg/15-lb cook control unless recipe specifies otherwise.

- If cooking different varieties together, check they all have the same cooking times.

COOKING TIMES

REMEMBER TO USE THE CORRECT AMOUNT OF LIQUID WHEN COOKING. THESE REQUIRE SLOW DEPRESSURISING.

BEANS, PEAS AND LENTILS

Variety	Cooking time
Aduki	5 minutes
Black beans	10 minutes
Black-eyed beans	10 minutes
Borlotti beans	10 minutes
Butter beans	15 minutes
Cannellini beans	10 minutes
Chick peas	20 minutes
Flageolet beans	5 minutes
Haricot beans – large	15 minutes
Haricot beans – small	10 minutes
Lentils – brown	3 minutes
Lentils – green	3 minutes
Lentils – red, no soak	Just bring to pressure
Mung beans	Just bring to pressure
Peas – marrowfat	20 minutes
Peas – split	3 minutes
Peas – whole	5 minutes
Pinto beans	12 minutes
Red kidney beans	10 minutes
Soya beans	25 minutes

GUIDELINES FOR
MEAT AND POULTRY

ALL TIMES ARE FOR POT ROASTING PER 450 G/1 LB – USE 6.8-KG/15-LB COOK
CONTROL. REFER TO MANUFACTURER'S INSTRUCTIONS.

- Pork and poultry should always be defrosted before cooking.

- When making casseroles do not coat in seasoned flour but
  thicken at the end of cooking. This applies to all foods.

- When cooking meat from frozen, cut into smaller pieces before
  freezing then place in the open cooker and brown, keeping the
  heat lower than usual to prevent spitting. Add about 5 minutes to
  the cooking time or, if a joint, allow an extra 10 minutes per
  450 g/1 lb.

- It is possible to reheat frozen cooked casseroles. Do not use the
  trivet and add 300 ml/½ pint of liquid to the frozen food. Cook for
  8 to 10 minutes depending on meat size. Depressurize quickly
  then adjust the consistency of the sauce.

- Joints should be no larger than 1.5 kg/3 lb. Do not fill the cooker
  more than half-full when all the vegetables and liquid have been
  added.

- Prepare whole birds by washing thoroughly inside the cavity and
  truss smaller birds to make them easier to handle. Cut large
  birds into portions so that the steam can circulate freely.

COOKING TIMES

JOINT	FROM DEFROSTED	FROM FROZEN
Beef		
Topside	12 minutes	22 minutes
Brisket	30 minutes	30 minutes
Silverside	15 minutes	25 minutes
Lamb		
Boned and rolled breast	15 minutes	25 minutes
Boned and rolled shoulder	15 minutes	25 minutes
Neck	12 minutes	22 minutes
Pork		
Boned and rolled shoulder	15 minutes	do not cook from frozen
Loin	12 minutes	
BOILING		
Bacon/gammon	8 minutes	do not cook from frozen
Brisket	20 minutes	30 minutes

GUIDELINES FOR **FISH**

- Remove the fins and scales, and if necessary clean whole fish, then rinse thoroughly.

- Cook in the cooker with a minimum of 300 ml/½ pint cooking liquid. If using milk, cook on a medium setting then use the milk to make the accompanying sauce.

- Oil the trivet thoroughly before use and place the fish on top. The fish can be placed on a sheet of greaseproof paper or foil for ease of handling.

- Fish needs only a short cooking time, so time carefully and depressurize quickly unless cooking with milk, in which case the pressure should be released.

- If cooking fish from frozen add an extra 1 minute if the fish is whole or a thick steak, and add an extra 2 minutes if cooking by weight.

- For all white fish, such as haddock, cod or halibut –
    cook fillets for 3 to 4 minutes;
    cook steaks 4 to 5 minutes.
  This also includes hake, herring, salmon, trout, mackerel and turbot fillets. More delicate fish, such as sole and plaice fillets, take 3 minutes. Whole fish take around 5 to 7 minutes, depending on size.

GUIDELINES FOR **STEAMED PUDDINGS, DESSERTS AND PRESERVES**

The pressure cooker is ideal for cooking all types of steamed puddings, desserts and preserves. There are just a few guidelines to remember to ensure a perfect result every time.

- Any container used must be ovenproof and filled no more than two-thirds full.

- Ensure you oil the container well and place a small circle of greaseproof paper in the base. Cover with a double sheet of greaseproof paper with a pleat in the centre or a single sheet of foil and secure firmly.

- Pour 900 ml/1½ pints boiling water into the cooker with 2 tablespoons of lemon juice to prevent discoloration.

- All puddings must be presteamed in order to make the rising agent work. See individual recipes and refer to manufacturer's handbook.

- Depressurize slowly so the pudding does not collapse and sink.

- Milk puddings can be cooked in a pressure cooker, but make sure the heat is not too hot on the base or they can burn.

- Christmas or Plum Puddings can be cooked in the pressure cooker. Refer to manufacturer's instructions for specific cooking times.

- Preserves can be cooked in a much shorter time than with conventional cooking. The fruit is softened in the cooker under pressure then, once the sugar is added, the preserve is cooked without the lid. Refer to manufacturer's instructions for specific times. The same general guidelines apply to preserves whether cooked in a pressure cooker or in a conventional manner.

GUIDELINES FOR **VEGETABLES**   **COOKING TIMES**

Vegetables require very little cooking time in the pressure cooker, especially if you prefer not to overcook them. Some, such as asparagus, green beans and cabbage, are best steamed or cooked in a conventional pan.

- If you do cook green vegetables in a pressure cooker, however, add them to boiling water. Use the 6.8-kg/15-lb cook control and depressurize quickly.

- Save time and fuel by cooking a selection of vegetables together. Cut them into even-sized pieces, and use the separator and dividers.

- If liked, cook root vegetables on the trivet with 300 ml/½ pint water, bring to the boil, then place green vegetables in the separator, place on top of the trivet, close the lid and bring to pressure. Depressurize quickly.

How long you cook your vegetables is a matter of choice. The table that follows will give you crisp rather than well-cooked vegetables. If you like softer vegetables, just increase the cooking time slightly. Bear in mind that root vegetables need to be properly cooked.

REMEMBER TO USE THE CORRECT AMOUNT OF LIQUID WHEN COOKING. THESE REQUIRE SLOW DEPRESSURISING.

Variety	Cooking time
Asparagus – tied into small bundles	2 to 4 minutes, depending on age
Artichokes	6 to 8 minutes, depending on size
Artichokes – Jerusalem	4 to 5 minutes
Aubergine	2 to 4 minutes depending on size
Beans – broad, French, green	1 to 3 minutes depending on age
Beetroot	Do not peel and leave a small amount of stalk and root. Wash carefully and cook for 2 to 4 minutes
Broccoli	1 to 2 minutes
Cabbage – shredded	Just bring to pressure
Cabbage – red	3 minutes
Carrots	3 to 4 minutes
Cauliflower – florets	1 to 2 minutes
Celery – cut into short lengths	2 minutes
Corn on the cob	6 to 10 minutes, depending on size
Courgettes – cut into thick slices	Just bring to pressure
Fennel	2 to 4 minutes, depending if halved or sliced
Leeks, sliced	2 to 3 minutes
Okra	2 to 3 minutes
Onions – whole	3 to 4 minutes
Parsnips – sliced or halved	3 to 4 minutes
Potatoes – new, whole	4 minutes
Potatoes – cut into chunks	4 minutes
Spinach	Just bring to pressure, with a little water
Swede and yams	6 minutes
Sweet potatoes – sliced	4 to 5 minutes
Turnips	3 to 4 minutes
Winter squass	6 to 10 minutes depending on type and quantity

ADAPTING OTHER RECIPES

It is very easy to adapt your own recipes once you have become used to pressure cooking. First of all refer to the manufacturer's cookbook for a similar recipe to the timings and method of depressurizing and remember that pressure cooking time is usually about two-thirds less than normal cooking.

Use liquids that produce steam, such as stock, wine or milk. Do not use melted butter or oil except to brown foods first and ensure that you use the minimal amount.

An important note to remember is that the cooking time is determined by the size of the food, not the quantity. Joints of meat, on the other hand, are timed by weight.

Use a medium setting for rice, pasta, cereals, pulses, beetroot and milk or any other foods that will froth up during cooking.

For stews and casseroles, brown the meat in the open cooker first, then wipe the cooker clean afterwards so the food does not burn when under pressure.

Some foods such as cook-in sauces and commercial soups may stick on the base so add an extra 150 ml/$^1/_4$ pint of liquid.

Never thicken stews, casseroles, soups or any sauces before cooking under pressure, always afterwards. This can be done either with cornflour, beurre manié (a flour-and-butter paste) or mashed vegetables such as potatoes.

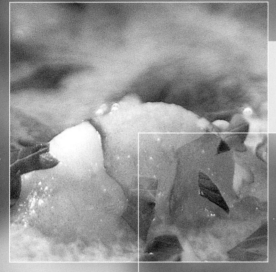

STOCKS
AND SOUPS

MEXICAN PINTO BEAN SOUP

IT IS IMPORTANT TO COVER THE DRIED BEANS WITH BOILING WATER AND SOAK 1 HOUR BEFORE PROCEEDING. COOKING BEANS IN THE PRESSURE COOKER ENSURES THAT ALL TOXINS ARE DESTROYED.

Place the beans in a large bowl, cover with boiling water, and leave for at least 1 hour. Drain then place in the cooker and add 600 ml/1 pint of water. Bring to the boil and remove any scum from the surface. Reduce the heat to a rolling boil and cover with the lid then bring to 6.8-kg/15-lb pressure.

Cook for 8 minutes then depressurize slowly. Remove the lid, lift out the beans from the cooker and reserve. Rinse and dry the cooker.

Heat the oil in the open cooker and sauté the chilli, garlic and onion for 5 minutes.

Add the contents of the can of tomatoes with the stock, oregano, seasoning to taste, the lime zest and juice and the reserved beans. Bring quickly back to the boil, cover with the lid and bring to 6.8-kg/15-lb pressure. Cook for 4 minutes.

Depressurize slowly, stir in the chopped coriander and adjust the seasoning to taste. Mix the chopped tomatoes and avocado together. Ladle the soup into individual serving bowls, add a spoonful of the soured cream and place a generous spoonful of the tomato and avocado on top.

Serves **6**
Cook control **6.8 kg/15 lb**
Preparation time **15 minutes**
   plus 1 hour soaking time
Open cooking time **8 minutes**
Pressure cooking time **12 minutes**

225 g/8 oz dried pinto beans
600 ml/1 pt water
1 Tbsp olive oil
1 red chilli, seeded and chopped
4 garlic cloves, peeled
   and chopped
1 onion, peeled and chopped
One 400-g/14-oz can chopped
   tomatoes

600 ml/1 pt vegetable or chicken
   stock
1 Tbsp chopped fresh oregano
Salt and freshly ground
   black pepper
Grated zest and juice of 1 lime
2 Tbsp chopped fresh coriander

TO SERVE

2 ripe tomatoes, peeled, seeded
   and chopped
1 small ripe avocado, peeled,
   stoned and finely diced
6 Tbsp soured cream

CHILLED WATERCRESS SOUP

THE SMALL AMOUNT OF CHILLI GIVES THIS CLASSIC SOUP A NEW TWIST. THE PIQUANT FLAVOUR IS DELICIOUS.

Wash the watercress, discarding any tough stalks, reserve a few sprigs for decoration and chop the remainder.

Melt the butter in the open cooker and sauté the onion, garlic, potatoes and crushed chillies for 5 minutes. Sprinkle in the flour and cook, stirring, for 1 minute.

Add the stock, chopped watercress and seasoning to taste, close the lid and bring to 6.8-kg/15-lb pressure. Cook for 4 minutes.

Depressurize quickly and adjust the seasoning. Cool slightly then purée in a food processor or blender. Allow to cool and stir in the soured cream. Chill then serve garnished with the reserved watercress sprigs.

Serves **6**
Cook control **6.8 kg/15 lb**
Preparation time **5 minutes,** plus chilling time
Open cooking time **4 minutes**
Pressure cooking time **4 minutes**

225 g/8 oz watercress
2 Tbsp unsalted butter
1 onion, peeled and chopped
1 to 2 garlic cloves, peeled and crushed
225 g/8 oz potatoes, peeled and diced
½ tsp dried crushed chillies
2 Tbsp white plain flour
900 ml/1½ pt vegetable or chicken stock
Salt and freshly ground black pepper
150 ml/¼ pt soured cream

WILD MUSHROOM SOUP

ANY DRIED WILD MUSHROOMS WILL WORK WELL IN THIS RECIPE.
REMEMBER TO USE THE SOAKING LIQUID AS WELL FOR MAXIMUM FLAVOUR.

Cover the dried mushrooms with almost-boiling water and soak for at least 20 minutes then drain, reserving the mushrooms and liquid.

Heat the oil in the open cooker and sauté the onions, garlic, chilli, potato and parsnip for 3 minutes, stirring frequently. Slice the mushrooms if large then add to the cooker and sauté for 1 minute. Add the stock and the rehydrated mushrooms with their soaking liquid, and bring to the boil.

Reduce the heat, close the lid and bring to 6.8-kg/15-lb pressure. Cook for 3 minutes then depressurize quickly and purée in batches in a blender.

Add seasoning to taste then reheat gently in the cleaned cooker before serving swirled with the cream or soured cream and sprinkled with the chives. Serve with warm crusty bread.

Serves **6**
Cook control **6.8 kg/15 lb**
Preparation time **10 minutes,**
   plus 20 minutes' soaking time
Open cooking time **5 minutes**
Pressure cooking time **3 minutes**

10 g/¼ oz dried mushrooms
1 Tbsp oil
2 medium onions, peeled
   and chopped
3 to 5 garlic cloves, peeled
   and chopped
1 red jalapeño chilli, seeded
   and finely chopped
1 potato, about 225 g/8 oz in
   weight, peeled and chopped

1 medium parsnip, about 175 g/
   6 oz, peeled and chopped
350 g/12 oz assorted fresh
   mushrooms, such as
   chanterelle, oyster, morels,
   chestnut and button
   mushrooms, wiped
900 ml/1½ pt vegetable stock
Salt and freshly ground
   black pepper

TO GARNISH
4 Tbsp single or soured cream
   and 2 Tbsp snipped fresh chives

TO SERVE
Crusty bread

PRAWN CHOWDER

CHOWDERS CAN BE MADE WITH A WIDE COMBINATION OF INGREDIENTS. THIS RECIPE IS
EXTRA SPECIAL BECAUSE IT USES LARGE PRAWNS, SO IT IS IDEAL WHEN YOU ARE ENTERTAINING.

Serves **8**
Cook control **6.8 kg/15 lb**
Preparation time **10 minutes**
Open cooking time **10 minutes**
Pressure cooking time **3 minutes**

225 g/8 oz raw king prawns
2 Tbsp unsalted butter
225 g/8 oz unsmoked back bacon, chopped
1 onion, peeled and chopped
2 celery sticks, trimmed and chopped
225 g/8 oz potatoes, peeled and diced
1 bay leaf
900 ml/1½ pt fish or vegetable stock
3 Tbsp cornflour
150 ml/¼ pt milk
100 g/4 oz peeled large prawns, defrosted if frozen
100 g/4 oz sweetcorn kernels, defrosted if frozen
Salt and freshly ground black pepper
2 to 3 Tbsp single cream
2 Tbsp chopped fresh parsley

Remove the heads from the prawns and peel. Discard. Melt the butter in the open cooker and sauté the bacon, onion and celery for 5 minutes. Add the potatoes and continue to sauté for a further 3 minutes. Add the bay leaf, stock and prawns.

Close the lid, bring to 6.8 kg/15 lb pressure and cook for 3 minutes.

Depressurize quickly, stir then remove the bay leaf. Blend the cornflour with the milk and stir into the cooker. Stir over a gentle heat until the mixture comes to the boil. Add the remaining ingredients, season, simmer for 2 minutes then serve with crusty granary bread.

CARROT AND LENTIL SOUP

FOR A CHANGE SUBSTITUTE 300 ML/½ PINT OF THE STOCK WITH ORANGE JUICE AND ADD 2 TABLESPOONS OF GRATED ORANGE ZEST BEFORE BRINGING TO PRESSURE. GARNISH WITH EXTRA ORANGE ZEST.

Serves **4**
Cook control **6.8 kg/15 lb**
Preparation time **10 minutes**
Open cooking time **5 minutes**
Pressure cooking time **5 minutes**

1 Tbsp oil
1 medium onion, peeled and chopped
4 garlic cloves, peeled and chopped
450 g/1 lb carrots, peeled and chopped
75 g/3 oz red split lentils
1 tsp ground cumin
1 tsp ground coriander

1 bay leaf
900 ml/1½ pt vegetable stock, heated
  to almost boiling
Salt and freshly ground black pepper
2 Tbsp chopped fresh coriander
4 Tbsp low-fat, natural yoghurt
  or single cream

TO SERVE
Crusty bread or croutons

Heat the oil in the open cooker and sauté the onion, garlic and carrots for 3 minutes. Add the lentils, spices and bay leaf and cook for 1 minute.

Pour in the hot stock and bring to the boil. Close the lid and bring to 6.8-kg/15-lb pressure. Cook for 5 minutes. Depressurize slowly then discard the bay leaf.

Cool slightly then purée in the blender. Season to taste, add the chopped coriander and reheat gently.

Ladle into bowls and swirl a spoonful of yoghurt or cream on top. Alternatively stir the yoghurt or cream into the soup. Serve with crusty bread or croutons.

FISH STOCK

WHEN MAKING YOUR OWN STOCK IT IS VITAL THAT ALL THE INGREDIENTS ARE EXTREMELY FRESH OR THE FINISHED STOCK WILL BE IMPAIRED.

Makes about **600 ml/1 pint**
Cook control **6.8 kg/15 lb**
Preparation time **4 minutes**
Open cooking time **3 minutes**
Pressure cooking time
  10 minutes

1 cod's head or fish bones
  and trimmings
1 celery stick
2 bay leaves
A few fresh parsley sprigs
A few fresh thyme sprigs
1 onion, peeled and sliced
1 small carrot, peeled and sliced
10 peppercorns
Salt

Rinse the cod's head or bones and trimmings and place in the open cooker. Cut the celery in half and place the bay leaves, parsley and thyme sprigs on one half of the celery and place the second half on top. Tie securely and place in the cooker. Add the onion, carrot and peppercorns then pour in 1.2 litres/ 2 pints cold water.

Bring to the boil in the open cooker then remove any scum which floats to the top with a slotted spoon. Add salt.

Close the lid and bring to 6.8-kg/15-lb pressure. Cook for 10 minutes. Depressurize slowly.

Strain, adjust the seasoning and allow to cool. Use the same day.

If liked, the stock can be frozen once cool. Use half the amount of liquid if freezing then add more water after defrosting. Use within 3 months if frozen.

BEEF STOCK

IT IS AN EXCELLENT IDEA, ONCE THE STOCK IS MADE, TO FREEZE SOME FOR LATER USE. POUR INTO SMALL CONTAINERS OR ICE CUBE TRAYS AND OPEN-FREEZE. ONCE FROZEN SOLID, PACK IN HEAVY-DUTY FREEZER BAGS TO STORE. DO NOT FORGET TO LABEL.

Makes about **600 ml/1 pint**
Cook control **6.8 kg/15 lb**
Preparation time **4 minutes**
Open cooking time **3 minutes**
Pressure cooking time
  15 minutes

900 g/2 lb meat bones, from
  either raw or cooked meat
2 onions, peeled and chopped
2 carrots, peeled and chopped
½ small head fennel, chopped
  or 2 celery sticks, trimmed
  and chopped
10 peppercorns
1 bouquet garni
Salt

Wash the bones and chop into 7.5-cm/3-inch lengths. Place in the open cooker with 1.2 litres/2 pints water and bring to the boil.

Remove any scum that floats to the surface with a slotted spoon.

Add the chopped vegetables with the peppercorns and bouquet garni then bring to the boil, add salt and close the lid.

Cook at 6.8-kg/15-lb pressure and cook for 15 minutes. Depressurize slowly then strain and skim off any fat from the surface. Cool before using.

Once cool, cover and store in the refrigerator for up to 3 days. Boil vigorously before use.

If using raw bones you can brown them in the open cooker in a little oil first. Wipe the cooker clean before adding the remaining ingredients.

CHICKEN STOCK

ANY POULTRY CARCASS CAN BE USED TO MAKE STOCK, BUT DO NOT USE DIFFERENT BIRDS AT THE SAME TIME. BREAK THE CARCASS UP INTO SMALLER PIECES SO THE BONES SIT EASILY IN THE COOKER.

Break the carcass into smaller pieces and place in the open cooker with any skin and pieces of chicken meat. Add the onion, carrot and celery with the bay leaves and parsley. Add the cloves and peppercorns then pour in 1.2 litres/2 pints cold water.

Bring to the boil and remove any scum that floats to the surface with a slotted spoon. Add salt.

Close the lid and bring to 6.8-kg/15-lb pressure then cook for 10 minutes.

Depressurize slowly then strain, skim off any fat and adjust the seasoning. Cool then use as required. If not using the same day, cool and store in the refrigerator for up to 3 days. Boil vigorously before use.

If freezing, use half the amount of liquid then add more water when defrosted.

Makes about **600 ml/1 pint**
Cook control **6.8 kg/15 lb**
Preparation time **5 minutes**
Open cooking time **3 minutes**
Pressure cooking time **10 minutes**

Carcass of 1 cooked chicken
1 medium onion, peeled and sliced
1 medium carrot, peeled and sliced
2 celery sticks, trimmed and sliced
2 bay leaves
A few fresh parsley sprigs
2 whole cloves
A few whole white peppercorns
Salt

PESTO SOUP

PESTO HAS BECOME VERY POPULAR IN RECENT YEARS AND THIS SOUP TAKES THE IDEA A LITTLE FURTHER.
IF LIKED, SPRINKLE THE FINISHED SOUP WITH A FEW TOASTED PINE NUTS.

Trim the leeks, slice thinly and wash thoroughly. Heat the butter in the open cooker and sauté the leeks, garlic and fennel for 5 minutes.

Add the remaining vegetables with the lemon zest, 2 tablespoons of the basil, stock and seasoning. Close the lid and quickly bring to 6.8-kg/15-lb pressure. Cook for 6 minutes then depressurize quickly.

Take out a little of the cooked vegetables then purée the remainder in a food processor or blender. Stir in the reserved vegetables and remaining basil. Heat gently then serve with the Parmesan cheese.

Serves **6**
Cook control **6.8 kg/15 lb**
Preparation time **10 minutes**
Open cooking time **5 minutes**
Pressure cooking time **6 minutes**

3 leeks (about 350 g/12 oz)
2 Tbsp unsalted butter
3 garlic cloves, peeled and crushed
1 head fennel, trimmed and chopped
2 courgettes, trimmed, sliced, and cut into half-moon shapes
100 g/4 oz green beans, trimmed and chopped
3 medium tomatoes, chopped and seeded
1 Tbsp grated lemon zest
3 Tbsp chopped fresh basil
900 ml/ 1½ pt vegetable or chicken stock
Salt and freshly ground black pepper

TO SERVE
Grated Parmesan cheese

BEAN GAZPACHO

YOU CAN ALSO SERVE THIS SOUP WARM. AFTER BLENDING, REHEAT GENTLY UNTIL PIPING HOT, THEN STIR IN THE CHOPPED GREEN PEPPER, TOMATOES, CUCUMBER, VINEGAR, PARSLEY AND SEASONING. HEAT THROUGH BRIEFLY THEN SERVE.

Serves **6**
Cook control **6.8 kg/15 lb**
Preparation time **10 minutes**
   plus 1 hour soaking
Pressure cooking time
   10 minutes

225 g/8 oz dried cannellini beans
1 litre/ 1¾ pints vegetable stock
4 to 6 garlic cloves, peeled
1 white onion, peeled
   and chopped
1 serrano chilli, seeded and
   chopped

4 ripe but still firm tomatoes,
   seeded and finely chopped
One 5-cm/2-inch piece
   cucumber, peeled, seeded
   and finely chopped
1 small green pepper, seeded
   and finely chopped
2 Tbsp sherry vinegar
Salt and freshly ground pepper
2 Tbsp freshly chopped flat-leaf
   parsley

TO SERVE
Croutons

Place the cannellini beans in a bowl, cover with boiling water and leave for 1 hour. Drain and place in the open cooker with 900 ml/1½ pints of the stock, garlic, onion and chilli. Bring to the boil then close the lid and bring to 6.8-kg/15-lb pressure. Cook for 10 minutes then depressurize slowly.

Once cool purée in a blender if liked and chill.

When ready to serve, stir the chopped tomatoes, cucumber, green pepper, vinegar, seasoning to taste and the chopped parsley. Serve with croutons.

BORSCHT

BORSCHT HAS THE MOST WONDERFUL DEEP PURPLE-RED COLOUR. WITH THE ADDITION OF SOURED CREAM AND CHIVES A BOWL OF BORSCHT LOOKS AND TASTES ABSOLUTELY STUNNING.

Serves **4 to 6**
Cook control **6.8 kg/15 lb**
Preparation time **10 minutes**
Open cooking time **3 minutes**
Pressure cooking time
   8 minutes

675 g/1½ lb raw beetroot, peeled
2 medium onions, peeled and
   chopped
2 garlic cloves, peeled and
   chopped

900 ml/1½ pt vegetable or beef
   stock
300 ml/½ pt orange juice
5 to 6 Tbsp dry sherry
Salt and ground black pepper

TO GARNISH
Half-fat crème fraîche or soured
   cream and fresh chives

TO SERVE
Sliced brown bread and butter
   or warm French bread

Grate or dice the beetroot and place in the open cooker with the onion, garlic, stock and 150 ml/¼ pint of the orange juice then bring to a gentle boil. Close the lid and bring to 6.8-kg/15-lb pressure and cook for 8 minutes.

Depressurize quickly then strain through a sieve and add the remaining orange juice, sherry and seasoning to taste.

Either chill or reheat gently and serve in individual bowls topped with a spoonful of half-fat crème fraîche or soured cream and 2 chives arranged across the top. Serve with thinly sliced brown bread and butter if serving chilled or chunks of warm French bread if serving hot.

TOMATO AND CHICK PEA SOUP

WHEN THE WEATHER BEGINS TO GET COOLER, SOUP IS ALWAYS POPULAR. THE SMALL AMOUNT OF CHILLI WILL REMOVE ANY COLD WEATHER CHILLS.

Place the chick peas in a bowl and cover with boiling water, leave for 1 hour, then drain and place in the open cooker with 600 ml/1 pint water. Bring to the boil and remove any scum that rises to the surface with a slotted spoon. Reduce the heat to a gentle boil, close the lid, and bring to 6.8-kg/15-lb pressure.

Cook for 15 minutes then depressurize slowly. Strain the chick peas through a colander and reserve.

Rinse and dry the cooker.

Heat the oil in the open cooker and sauté the onion, chilli, garlic, red pepper and fennel for 3 minutes.

Add the chopped tomatoes with the oregano and the reserved chick peas.

Blend the tomato purée with the stock and vinegar and pour into the cooker. Bring back to the boil then close the lid and bring to 6.8-kg/15-lb pressure. Cook for 5 minutes then depressurize quickly and add seasoning to taste with the shredded basil.

Serves **6**
Cook control **6.8 kg/15 lb**
Preparation time **10 minutes plus 1 hour soaking time**
Open cooking time **3 minutes**
Pressure cooking time **20 minutes**

175 g/6 oz dried chick peas

1 Tbsp oil

1 medium onion, peeled and chopped

1 jalapeño chilli, seeded and chopped

3 garlic cloves, peeled and chopped

1 small red pepper, seeded and chopped

½ small head fennel, trimmed and chopped

350 g/12 oz ripe tomatoes, chopped

1 Tbsp chopped fresh oregano

2 Tbsp tomato purée

600 ml/1 pt vegetable stock

1 Tbsp red wine vinegar

Salt and freshly ground black pepper

2 Tbsp shredded basil

ROASTED RED PEPPER SOUP

THE PEPPERS CAN BE ROASTED EITHER IN THE OVEN OR UNDER A PREHEATED GRILL. ROASTING TAKES MUCH LONGER BUT GIVES A MORE INTENSE FLAVOUR. CHARRING UNDER THE GRILL OR IN THE COOKER IS MUCH QUICKER.

Heat 2 teaspoons of the oil in the open cooker, add the red peppers and sauté for 8 minutes or until the skins have begun to char. Remove from the cooker with a slotted spoon, chop, and reserve. Wipe the pan clean.

Add the remaining oil with the garlic and onion and sauté for 3 minutes. Return the chopped peppers to the pan with the tomatoes, saffron, shredded basil and stock. Add seasoning to taste and bring to the boil. Close the lid and quickly bring to 6.8-kg/15-lb pressure. Cook for 6 minutes then quickly depressurize.

Purée the soup in a blender, rub through a fine sieve and adjust the seasoning. If serving warm, return to the rinsed cooker and heat gently. If serving cold, chill until required. Swirl with the cream or crème fraîche and serve garnished with the shredded basil and croutons.

Serves **6**
Cook control **6.8 kg/15 lb**
Preparation time **10 minutes**
Open cooking time **11 minutes**
Pressure cooking time **6 minutes**

2 Tbsp olive oil
3 red peppers, seeded and quartered
3 garlic cloves, peeled and crushed
1 onion, peeled and chopped
450 g/1 lb large ripe tomatoes, chopped
A few strands saffron
1 Tbsp shredded basil leaves
900 ml/1½ pints vegetable or
  chicken stock
Salt and freshly ground black pepper
4 Tbsp single cream or half-fat
  crème fraîche

TO GARNISH
1 Tbsp shredded basil
Garlic croutons

POTATO AND SPINACH
VICHYSSOISE

THIS SOUP IS DELICIOUS SERVED EITHER WARM OR CHILLED. IF CHILLING, COOL AS QUICKLY AS POSSIBLE THEN CHILL IN THE REFRIGERATOR FOR AT LEAST 4 HOURS.

Serves **4 to 6**
Cook control **6.8 kg/15 lb**
Preparation time **7 minutes**
Open cooking time **5 minutes**
Pressure cooking time **6 minutes**

1 Tbsp oil
1 medium onion, peeled and
  chopped
3 garlic cloves, peeled and
  chopped
300 g/10 oz potatoes, peeled
  and diced

1 large leek, about 225 g/8 oz in
  weight, trimmed and sliced
900 ml/1½ pints vegetable stock
2 Tbsp grated lemon zest
3 sprigs fresh dill
225 g/8 oz fresh spinach
Salt and freshly ground black
  pepper
150 ml/¼ pint single cream or
  full-cream milk

TO GARNISH
2 Tbsp chopped fresh dill

Heat the oil in the open cooker and sauté the onion, garlic, potatoes and leek for 3 minutes. Add the stock, lemon zest and dill sprigs and bring to a gentle boil.

Close the lid and bring to 6.8-kg/15-lb pressure. Cook for 5 minutes then depressurize quickly.

Meanwhile discard any tough outer leaves and stems from the spinach, wash thoroughly and chop. Open the cooker and add the spinach. Close the lid and return to pressure. Cook for 1 minute then depressurize quickly.

Purée in a blender, adjust the seasoning then stir in the cream or milk. Reheat gently in the cleaned, open cooker for 2 minutes or until almost at boiling point, then serve sprinkled with the chopped dill.

VEGETABLE STOCK

WHEN MAKING VEGETABLE STOCK DO NOT USE STARCHY FOODS OR GREEN VEGETABLES BECAUSE THEY WILL MAKE THE STOCK CLOUDY. IF LIKED, THE ONION SKINS CAN BE INCLUDED TO GIVE A DARKER STOCK. REMEMBER THAT ALL HOME-MADE STOCKS ARE AT THEIR BEST IF FRESHLY MADE. FREEZING LOSES A LITTLE OF THE FLAVOUR.

Makes about **600 ml/1 pint**
Cook control **6.8 kg/15 lb**
Preparation time **5 minutes**
Open cooking time **3 minutes**
Pressure cooking time
  10 minutes

2 onions, peeled and chopped
2 garlic cloves, peeled and
  chopped

1 large carrot, peeled and
  chopped
2 celery sticks, trimmed and
  chopped
1 small turnip, peeled and
  chopped
2 bay leaves
1 bouquet garni
5 peppercorns
Salt

Place the chopped vegetables in the open cooker with the bay leaves, bouquet garni and peppercorns. Pour in 1.2 litres/2 pints cold water and bring to the boil. Remove any scum that floats to the surface with a slotted spoon and then add salt.

Close the lid and bring to 6.8-kg/15-lb pressure. Cook for 30 minutes. Depressurize quickly.

Strain the stock and allow to cool before using. Store in the refrigerator for up to 3 days. Boil vigorously before using.

If freezing, use half the quantity of water, freeze for up to 3 months and, once defrosted, add the remaining water.

FISH

SALMON WITH MUSHROOM SAUCE

FRESH SALMON STEAKS ARE AS EASY TO COOK AS THEY ARE DELICIOUS.

Melt the 2 tablespoons of butter in the open cooker and gently sauté the shallots for 3 minutes. Add the mushrooms and continue to sauté for 2 minutes then pour in the wine.

Brush the trivet with the melted butter and place the salmon steaks on a sheet of greaseproof paper and place on the trivet. Place rim-side down into the cooker.

Tie the asparagus into small bundles and place greaseproof paper on top of the salmon. Place the asparagus bundles on top. Close the lid and bring to 6.8-kg/15-lb pressure. Cook for 3 minutes.

Depressurize quickly then remove the asparagus and salmon and keep warm. Blend the cornflour with the cream and stir into the liquid remaining in the cooker.

Cook, stirring until the sauce thickens. Add seasoning to taste then pour over the salmon. Serve scattered with the spring onions and dill.

Serves **4**
Cook control **6.8 kg/15 lb**
Preparation time **10 minutes**
Open cooking time **5 minutes**
Pressure cooking time **3 minutes**

2 Tbsp unsalted butter plus 1 tsp melted butter

4 shallots, peeled and sliced into thin wedges

75 g/3 oz button mushrooms, wiped and sliced

75 g/3 oz oyster mushrooms, wiped and chopped if large

300 ml/½ pt dry white wine

Four 150-g/5-oz salmon steaks, wiped

225 g/8 oz baby asparagus tips, rinsed

1 tsp cornflour

3 Tbsp single cream

Salt and freshly ground black pepper

TO GARNISH

4 spring onions, trimmed and diagonally sliced

2 Tbsp chopped fresh dill

SPINACH AND PINE NUT-
STUFFED SOLE

PLAICE CAN BE USED INSTEAD OF SOLE IN THIS RECIPE IF PREFERRED.

Heat the oil in the open cooker and sauté the shallots for 3 minutes. Place in a bowl and wipe the cooker clean. Add the remaining stuffing ingredients to the shallots with seasoning to taste and mix to a stiff consistency with the beaten egg.

Lightly rinse or wipe the fish fillets with absorbent kitchen paper and set aside. Discard any tough stalks from the spinach, rinse well then place in a bowl and pour over boiling water to cover. Leave for 1 to 2 minutes until pliable, then drain well.

Place the fillets skin-side down on a chopping board and place 2 to 3 spinach leaves on top. Divide the stuffing among the 4 fish fillets, gently spread over each fillet then roll up starting from the tail end. Secure with cocktail sticks.

Lightly oil the trivet and place rim-side down in the cooker. Place the fish on top. Mix the wine with the lemon juice and 150 ml/¼ pint water and pour over the fish. Close the lid and bring to 6.8-kg/15-lb pressure. Cook for 3 minutes then depressurize quickly.

Lift the fish out of the cooker and keep warm. Strain the liquid and return it to the cooker. Blend the butter or margarine and flour to form a paste. Bring the liquid remaining in the cooker to the boil then whisk in small spoonfuls of the paste. Cook, stirring, until a smooth glossy sauce is formed. Roughly chop the prawns and add to the sauce with the cream. Season to taste. Pour over the fish, garnish and serve.

Serves **4**
Cook control **6.8 kg/15 lb**
Preparation time **20 minutes**
Open cooking time **6 minutes**
Pressure cooking time **3 minutes**

FOR THE STUFFING
1 Tbsp oil
3 shallots, peeled and finely chopped
6 spring onions, trimmed and
   chopped
1 Tbsp grated lemon zest
2 Tbsp toasted pine kernels
50 g/2 oz button mushrooms,
   chopped
75 g/3 oz fresh white breadcrumbs
Salt and ground black pepper

1 medium egg, beaten

FOR THE FISH
4 large sole fillets, skinned
8 to 12 large spinach leaves
150 ml/¼ pt medium-dry
   white wine
2 Tbsp lemon juice
2 tsp softened butter
   or margarine
2 tsp white plain flour
50 g/2 oz peeled prawns,
   defrosted if frozen
3 Tbsp single cream

TO GARNISH
Fresh herbs and lemon wedges

SPICY FISH STEAKS

USE A FIRM FISH FOR THIS RECIPE. FISH SUCH AS PLAICE OR SOLE WOULD BE TOO DELICATE AND THEIR FLAVOUR WOULD BE COMPLETELY OVERPOWERED. MARINATE THE FISH IN THE REFRIGERATOR FOR SEVERAL HOURS TO INTENSIFY THE SPICY FLAVOUR.

Wipe the fish steaks with absorbent kitchen paper and set aside. Mix the spices with seasoning to taste and about 1 tablespoon of oil to form a thick paste then brush over the fish steaks. Place on a plate, cover loosely and leave in the refrigerator for at least 1 hour, overnight if time permits.

Heat the remaining oil in the open cooker and sauté the onion, garlic and aubergine for 2 minutes. Add the courgette and red pepper and sauté for a further 2 minutes. Add the tomatoes, seasoning and 1 tablespoon of the chopped coriander and pour over the tomato juice.

Place the fish steaks on top and close the lid. Bring to 6.8-kg/15-lb pressure and cook for 3 minutes. Depressurize quickly, then lift out the fish steaks and vegetables using a slotted spoon and place in a serving dish. Keep warm.

Blend the cornflour with 1 tablespoon water and stir into the juices left in the cooker. Cook, stirring until the sauce thickens, adjust the seasoning and pour over the fish. Garnish with the remaining coriander and serve with fresh cooked rice.

Serves **4**
Cook control **6.8 kg/15 lb**
Preparation time **10 minutes**
Open cooking time **5 minutes**
Pressure cooking time **3 minutes**

Four 150-g/5-oz fish steaks, such as swordfish, cod or haddock
1 tsp ground coriander
1 tsp ground cumin
½ to 1 tsp chilli powder
Salt and freshly ground black pepper
2 Tbsp oil
1 onion, peeled and chopped
3 to 4 garlic cloves, peeled and crushed

1 small aubergine, about 225 g/ 8 oz, trimmed and diced
2 medium courgettes, trimmed and cut into large dice
1 red pepper, seeded and cut into half-moon slices
4 ripe but firm tomatoes, seeded if preferred and cut into quarters
2 Tbsp chopped fresh coriander
250 ml/8 fl oz tomato juice
2 tsp cornflour

TO SERVE
Rice

COCONUT-FLAVOURED HADDOCK

THE COCONUT IN THIS DISH ADDS A BEAUTIFULLY CREAMY FLAVOUR. IF YOU CANNOT FIND COCONUT MILK EASILY IN YOUR LOCAL STORES, SOAK SOME DESICCATED COCONUT IN ALMOST-BOILING WATER FOR 20 MINUTES, STRAIN, THEN USE THE FLAVOURED WATER.

Wipe the fish fillets and place on a sheet of greaseproof paper. Brush the trivet with the melted butter and place rim-side down into the cooker. Place the fish on the paper onto the trivet and sprinkle with the saffron and the coconut milk. Roughly chop 3 of the spring onions and scatter on top of the fish.

Line the separator with foil and add the rice, 450 ml/³/₄ pint boiling water, sweetcorn and apricots. Finely chop the remaining spring onions and chilli and add to the rice. Place on top of the fish.

Close the lid and bring to 4.5 kg/10 lb pressure. Cook for 5 minutes. Depressurize slowly and lift out the rice and the fish.

Flake the fish into bite-sized pieces and stir into the rice with salt and paprika to taste. Add the chopped coriander, stir lightly then serve.

Serves **4**
Cook control **4.5 kg/10 lb**
Preparation time **15 minutes**
Pressure cooking time
  5 minutes

4 pieces haddock fillet
1 tsp melted butter
A few saffron strands

300 ml/½ pt coconut milk
8 spring onions, trimmed
300 g/10 oz basmati rice
100 g/4 oz sweetcorn kernels
75 g/3 oz dried apricots, chopped
1 red chilli, seeded and chopped
Salt
Paprika
2 Tbsp chopped fresh coriander

PROVENÇAL COD LOIN

COD LOIN IS MORE EXPENSIVE THAN FILLET OR CUTLETS,
BUT WELL WORTH THE PRICE BECAUSE YOU GET FIRM, THICK PIECES
OF FISH WITH VERY FEW IF ANY BONES.

Serves **4**
Cook control **6.8 kg/15 lb**
Preparation time **5 minutes**
Open cooking time **5 minutes**
Pressure cooking time **3 minutes**

1 Tbsp oil
1 onion, peeled and sliced
4 garlic cloves, peeled and sliced
3 celery sticks, trimmed and sliced
1 green pepper, seeded and sliced
1 red pepper, seeded and sliced
2 courgettes, trimmed and sliced

One 400-g/14-oz can chopped tomatoes
1 Tbsp tomato purée
1 Tbsp chopped fresh oregano
Four 150-g/5-oz pieces cod loin
1 tsp cornflour
Salt and freshly ground black pepper

TO GARNISH
50 g/2 oz stoned black olives, chopped
1 Tbsp chopped fresh oregano

TO SERVE
Potatoes or rice, and vegetables

Heat the oil in the open cooker and sauté the onion, garlic, celery and peppers for
3 minutes or until just beginning to soften. Add the courgettes and chopped
tomatoes with their juice. Blend the tomato purée with 150 ml/¹/₄ pint water and
add to the cooker with the oregano. Place the cod on top.

Close the lid and bring to 6.8-kg/15-lb pressure. Cook for 3 minutes. Depressurize
quickly then lift out the fish and keep warm.

Blend the cornflour with 1 tablespoon of water and stir into the sauce. Bring to
the boil and cook, stirring until thickened, then add seasoning to taste.

Pour the sauce over the fish and sprinkle with the chopped olives and oregano.
Serve with freshly cooked potatoes or rice, and vegetables.

PROVENÇAL COD LOIN

TROUT WITH HERB BUTTER

IF YOU CANNOT FIND SMALL WHOLE TROUT THAT WILL FIT IN YOUR PRESSURE COOKER, USE TROUT FILLETS INSTEAD AND COOK FOR JUST 2 MINUTES.

Serves **4**
Cook control **6.8 kg/15 lb**
Preparation time **8 minutes**
Pressure cooking time **3 minutes**

FOR THE BUTTER

1 lemon
75 g/3 oz butter, softened
1 Tbsp chopped fresh parsley
1 Tbsp chopped fresh dill
1 Tbsp snipped fresh chives

FOR THE FISH

4 small 225-g/8-oz trout, cleaned
Salt and freshly ground black pepper
1 medium onion, peeled and sliced
4 bay leaves
3 celery sticks, trimmed and chopped
300 ml/½ pt equal parts white wine and water mixed together

TO GARNISH

Lemon wedges and fresh herb sprigs

TO SERVE

New potatoes and vegetables and/or salad

Grate the zest from the lemon, reserve the zest and thinly slice the lemon. Cream the softened butter with the lemon zest and chopped herbs, shape into a roll, wrap in greaseproof paper and chill in the refrigerator until required.

Rinse the trout and pat dry with absorbent kitchen paper. Season the cavities with salt and pepper and place a little of the sliced onion in each fish cavity with a bay leaf. Place half a slice of lemon in each cavity and press the flesh together.

Place the remaining onion, sliced lemon and chopped celery in the open cooker and place the trout on top. Pour over the wine and water and close the lid.

Bring to 6.8-kg/15-lb pressure and cook for 3 minutes. Depressurize quickly then remove the trout from the cooker. Place a quarter of the herb butter on top of each fish and garnish with lemon wedges and herb sprigs. Serve with new potatoes and fresh cooked vegetables and/or salad.

WARM TUNA AND PASTA SALAD

IF FRESH TUNA IS UNAVAILABLE, USE SWORDFISH OR SALMON STEAKS INSTEAD. TAKE CARE NOT TO OVERCOOK FRESH TUNA OR IT WILL BECOME DRY AND TASTELESS.

Heat the oil in the open cooker and sauté the onion, chilli and celery for 3 minutes, add the chopped peppers with the aubergine and continue to sauté for 4 minutes. Add the chopped tomatoes with their juice and the black olives.

Lightly oil the trivet then place it rim-side down into the cooker. Place the tuna steaks on top.

Line the separator with foil, add the pasta and 450 ml/³/₄ pint water and place on top of the tuna. Close the lid, bring to 6.8-kg/15-lb pressure and cook for 5 minutes. Depressurize quickly and lift out the pasta and tuna. Drain the pasta, place into a bowl and stir. Flake the tuna into bite-sized pieces and add to the pasta together with the cooked vegetables. Season to taste. Stir lightly then serve warm, sprinkled with the shredded basil and shavings of Parmesan cheese, if using.

Serves **6**
Cook control **6.8 kg/15 lb**
Preparation time **10 minutes**
Open cooking time **7 minutes**
Pressure cooking time **5 minutes**

1 Tbsp olive oil
1 onion, peeled and cut into wedges
1 small jalapeño chilli, seeded and chopped
3 celery sticks, trimmed and sliced
1 red pepper, seeded and chopped
1 green pepper, seeded and chopped
1 small aubergine, trimmed and chopped
One 400-g/14-oz can chopped tomatoes
100 g/4 oz stoned black olives
450 g/1 lb fresh tuna steak
Generous 175 g/6 oz dried pasta shapes such as farfalle or twists
Salt and freshly ground black pepper

TO GARNISH
2 Tbsp shredded basil

TO SERVE
Shavings of Parmesan cheese (optional)

SMOKED HADDOCK PILAF

I ALWAYS USE UNDYED SMOKED HADDOCK BECAUSE, IN MY OPINION, THE FLAVOUR IS FAR SUPERIOR, BUT IT IS A QUESTION OF PERSONAL TASTE, SO USE WHICHEVER YOU PREFER. THIS RECIPE WILL WORK WELL WITH EITHER.

Pour 300 ml/½ pint of water into the pressure cooker and place the trivet in, rim-side down. Line the separator with foil, add the peas and rice and pour over 450 ml/¾ pint of the stock. Close the lid and bring to 6.8-kg/15-lb pressure and cook for 5 minutes. Depressurize slowly then remove the peas and rice and keep warm. Remove the trivet and wipe the cooker clean.

Heat the oil in the open cooker and sauté the bacon, onion, garlic and celery for 3 minutes. Stir in the red pepper, mushrooms, chopped tomatoes and the remaining stock and place the fish on top.

Close the lid and bring to 6.8-kg/15-lb pressure and cook for 5 minutes. Depressurize quickly then lift out the separator and transfer to a warm serving dish. Flake the fish into bite-sized pieces and mix into the cooked rice with the vegetables. Add seasoning to taste. Serve immediately, garnished with the parsley sprigs.

Serves **4**
Cook control **6.8 kg/15 lb**
Preparation time **15 minutes**
Open cooking time **3 minutes**
Pressure cooking time
  10 minutes

75 g/3 oz frozen peas
225 g/8 oz long-grain rice
600 ml/1 pt fish or vegetable stock
1 Tbsp oil
225 g/8 oz smoked bacon, chopped
1 medium onion, peeled and
  chopped
3 garlic cloves, peeled
  and chopped

3 celery sticks, trimmed
  and chopped
1 red pepper, seeded
  and chopped
4 large field mushrooms,
  trimmed and chopped
One 400-g/14-oz can chopped
  tomatoes
350 g/12 oz smoked haddock
  fillet, skinned
Salt and freshly ground
  black pepper

TO GARNISH
Flat-leaf parsley sprigs

ORIENTAL SEA BASS

IF YOU CAN FIND SMALL WHOLE SEA BASS THAT WILL FIT INTO THE PRESSURE COOKER, USE THEM. OTHERWISE, USE FILLETS TO ENSURE THAT THE FISH IS DONE AND LOOKS ATTRACTIVE WHEN SERVED.

Rinse the fish, pat dry and reserve. Mix together the grated ginger, garlic, lemon grass and chilli. Place in the fish cavity or on the fillets and roll up loosely then top with the star anise and the shredded spring onions.

Lightly oil the trivet, set it in the cooker rim-side down and place the fish on top. Mix the stock with the sake or sherry and pour over the fish.

Line the separator with foil and add the rice then pour in 450 ml/³/₄ pint boiling water. Place in the cooker on top of the fish. Close the lid and bring quickly to 6.8-kg/15-lb pressure. Cook for 5 minutes.

Depressurize quickly then remove the rice and fish and keep warm. Strain the cooking liquid, return it to the cleaned cooker and bring to the boil. Blend the cornflour with 1 tablespoon of water then stir into the boiling liquid. Cook, stirring until thickened.

Arrange the rice on warm individual serving plates, top with the fish, pour over a little of the sauce and serve the remainder separately. Garnish with coriander sprigs and serve immediately, with the salad.

Serves **4**
Cook control **6.8 kg/15 lb**
Preparation time **10 minutes**
Pressure cooking time **5 minutes**

4 small whole sea bass or four 225-g/8-oz sea bass or similar fish fillets, cleaned and descaled if necessary
One 5-cm/2-in piece fresh root ginger, peeled and grated
2 large garlic cloves, peeled and crushed
3 lemon grass stalks, outer leaves discarded and very finely chopped
1 serrano chilli, seeded and finely chopped

8 star anise
6 large spring onions, trimmed and shredded
1 tsp oil
250 ml/8 fl oz fish or vegetable stock
50 ml/2 fl oz sake or dry sherry
300 g/10 oz fragrant Thai rice
1 tsp cornflour

TO GARNISH
Coriander sprigs

TO SERVE
Chinese-style green leaf salad

NAVARIN OF MONKFISH
WITH SPRING VEGETABLES

MONKFISH MAY LOOK VERY UGLY BUT ITS FIRM FLESH MAKES IT A SUPERB FISH TO COOK WITH AND ONE THAT WORKS WELL WITH ROBUST FLAVOURS.

Discard the central bone and any skin from the monkfish, rinse lightly then cut into small pieces. Season well and set aside. Cut all the root vegetables into even-sized pieces and set aside.

Heat the oil in the open cooker and gently sauté the vegetables except the broad beans and courgettes for 3 minutes. Add the beans and courgettes and sauté for 1 minute then add the bouquet garni to the cooker.

Blend the tomato purée with the stock, then pour over the vegetables and add a little seasoning. Place the fish pieces on top and sprinkle with 1 tablespoon of the dill. Close the lid and bring to 6.8-kg/15-lb pressure. Cook for 3 minutes.

Depressurize quickly then adjust the seasoning and remove the cooked vegetables and fish and keep warm.

Blend the butter and flour together to form a paste then whisk small spoonfuls into the liquid remaining in the cooker. Bring to the boil, whisking, and cook until thickened. Pour over the fish and vegetables then serve sprinkled with the remaining chopped dill.

Serves **4**
Cook control **6.8 kg/15 lb**
Preparation time **20 minutes**
Open cooking time **4 minutes**
Pressure cooking time **3 minutes**

One 675-g/1½-lb piece monkfish tail
Salt and freshly ground black pepper
8 baby onions, peeled
4 baby turnips, peeled
300 g/10 oz baby potatoes, scrubbed
300 g/10 oz baby carrots, scrubbed
1 Tbsp oil
1 cup shelled broad beans
175 g/6 oz baby courgettes, trimmed
1 bouquet garni
2 Tbsp tomato purée
300 ml/½ pt vegetable stock
2 Tbsp chopped fresh dill
1 Tbsp softened butter
1 Tbsp white plain flour

MEAT

SWEET-AND-SOUR PORK
WITH PINEAPPLE

WHETHER YOU ARE COOKING FOR THE FAMILY OR ENTERTAINING FRIENDS, THIS COLOURFUL PORK DISH IS AN IDEAL CHOICE. BY USING YOUR PRESSURE COOKER, YOU CAN HAVE IT READY IN MINUTES.

Heat the oil in the open cooker then sauté the pork for 5 minutes or until sealed. Remove with a slotted spoon and reserve. Add the onions and garlic and sauté for 5 minutes or until softened. Remove and drain off any excess oil.

Return the pork and onions to the cooker with the carrots, pepper strips and mushrooms.

Drain the juice from the pineapple and set aside the pineapple. Make the juice up to 300 ml/½ pint with water. Blend the ketchup, soy sauce, vinegar and sugar together then stir in the pineapple juice and pour in the cooker.

Close the lid, bring to 6.8-kg/15 -lb pressure quickly and cook for 5 minutes. Depressurize quickly then stir in the reserved pineapple.

Blend the cornflour with 1 tablespoon water and stir into the cooker. Bring to the boil, stirring until thickened. Add seasoning to taste, sprinkle with the cashews and parsley and serve with the rice or potatoes.

Serves **4**
Cook control **6.8 kg/15 lb**
Preparation time **15 minutes**
Open cooking time **15 minutes**
Pressure cooking time **5 minutes**

1 Tbsp oil
450 g/1 lb pork fillet, trimmed and cubed
2 red onions, peeled and cut into wedges
4 garlic cloves, peeled and sliced
225 g/8 oz carrots, peeled and cut into thin strips
1 red pepper, seeded and cut into strips
1 yellow pepper, seeded and cut into strips
100 g/ 4 oz wild or button mushrooms, wiped and sliced if large
One 200-g/7-oz can pineapple pieces
2 Tbsp ketchup
1 Tbsp light soy sauce
1 Tbsp white wine vinegar
2 tsp soft brown sugar
1 Tbsp cornflour
Salt and freshly ground black pepper
50 g/2 oz cashews, toasted

TO GARNISH
1 Tbsp chopped fresh flat-leaf parsley

TO SERVE
Rice or new potatoes

BARBECUED PORK RIBS

PROVIDE PLENTY OF PAPER NAPKINS AND SOME FINGER BOWLS FOR YOUR GUESTS
WHEN SERVING THESE DELICIOUS RIBS.

Serves **4**
Cook control **6.8 kg/15 lb**
Preparation time **5 minutes**
Open cooking time **10 minutes**
Pressure cooking time **10 minutes**

2 Tbsp oil
900 g/2 lb Chinese-style pork ribs
1 large onion, peeled and chopped
4 to 6 garlic cloves, peeled and crushed
4 celery sticks, trimmed and sliced
2 Tbsp tomato purée
1 Tbsp Dijon mustard
1 Tbsp black treacle
4 Tbsp light soft brown sugar
250 ml/8 fl oz chicken or vegetable stock
175 g/6 oz cherry tomatoes

TO SERVE
Shredded Bok Choi or similar
  Asian leaf

Heat 1 tablespoon of the oil in the open cooker and brown the ribs on all sides. Remove from the cooker and set aside. Clean the pan then add the remaining oil and add the onion, garlic and celery to the cooker. Sauté for 5 minutes then return the ribs to the cooker.

Blend the tomato purée, mustard, treacle, sugar and stock and pour over the ribs. Add the cherry tomatoes and close the lid.

Bring the cooker to 6.8-kg/15-lb pressure and cook for 10 minutes. Depressurize quickly and either serve immediately on a bed of shredded Asian leaves or arrange on a foil-lined grill pan and cook under a preheated grill for 10 minutes, turning over at least once, until the ribs are crisp.

PORK AND APRICOT CASSEROLE

DRIED APRICOTS ARE ONE OF MY ALL-TIME FAVOURITE INGREDIENTS AND THEY FEATURE IN MANY OF MY DISHES. HERE I HAVE COMBINED THEM WITH CIDER TO GIVE THE PORK AN UNUSUAL, INTERESTING FLAVOUR.

Serves **4**
Cook control **6.8 kg/15 lb**
Preparation time **10 minutes**
Open cooking time **6 minutes**
Pressure cooking time
  15 minutes

450 g/1 lb pork tenderloin
1 Tbsp oil
1 medium onion, peeled and sliced
3 to 4 garlic cloves, peeled and sliced
75 g/3 oz dried apricots, chopped
2 medium carrots, peeled and cut
  into batons
1 yellow pepper, seeded and cut into half
  moon shapes
1 bouquet garni
450 ml/¾ sweet cider
1 Tbsp dark soy sauce
Salt and freshly ground black pepper
2 tsp cornflour

TO GARNISH
Fresh apricots, if available, and fresh
  sage leaves

TO SERVE
Freshly cooked vegetables

Trim off any fat from the pork and cut into small pieces. Heat the oil in the open cooker and sauté the onion, garlic, apricots and carrots for 2 minutes. Remove from the cooker with a slotted spoon and reserve. Add the pork to the cooker and cook, stirring for 2 minutes or until sealed.

Return the onion mixture to the cooker and add the yellow pepper and bouquet garni then pour in the cider. Stir well.

Close the lid and bring to 6.8-kg/15-lb pressure. Cook for 15 minutes. Depressurize quickly then add soy sauce with seasoning to taste. Blend the cornflour with 1 tablespoon of extra cider or water and stir into the open cooker. Place over a gentle heat and cook, stirring until slightly thickened. Remove the bouquet garni and garnish with apricots and sage. Serve with freshly cooked vegetables.

PORK WITH PRUNE
AND ORANGE STUFFING

YOU HAVE TO ADOPT A SLIGHTLY DIFFERENT ATTITUDE TO SEASONING WHEN COOKING
WITH A PRESSURE COOKER. I HAVE FOUND THAT UNLESS YOU USE PLENTY OF SEASONING
THE FOOD CAN BE QUITE BLAND, SO ADD SEASONING BEFORE COOKING, BUT ALWAYS CHECK
AND ADJUST AFTERWARDS, BEFORE SERVING.

Cut along the length of the pork chops along the fat edge
to form a pocket.

Heat the oil in the open cooker and brown the chops on all
sides (you may need to do this in 2 batches). Remove from
the cooker and cool while preparing the stuffing.

Mix together the chopped prunes, orange zest, pecans, rice
and sage with seasoning, stir in the egg yolk then stuff the
pork chops with the mixture.

Place the pork chops in the cooker and add the orange juice
and white wine.

Close the lid and bring to 6.8-kg/15-lb pressure. Cook for 15
minutes. Depressurize quickly then remove from the cooker
and keep warm.

Add the orange jelly marmalade to the liquid remaining in the
cooker, bring to the boil and boil for 2 to 3 minutes or until
the sauce becomes syrupy. Pour the sauce over the chops and
garnish with the fresh sage leaves and sliced plums. Serve
with freshly cooked vegetables or salad.

Serves **4**
Cook control **6.8 kg/15 lb**
Preparation time **10 minutes**
Open cooking time **8 minutes**
Pressure cooking time
  15 minutes

4 boneless pork chops
1 Tbsp oil
50 g/2 oz dried prunes, chopped
1 Tbsp grated orange zest
2 Tbsp pecans, chopped
50 g/2 oz cooked long-grain rice
1 Tbsp chopped fresh sage

Salt and freshly ground black
  pepper
1 small egg yolk
150 ml/¼ pt orange juice
150 ml/¼ pt dry white wine
2 Tbsp orange jelly marmalade

TO GARNISH
Fresh sage leaves and sliced
  fresh plums

TO SERVE
Vegetables or salad

PAPRIKA PORK

COMFORT FOOD IS ALWAYS APPRECIATED WHEN THE WEATHER TURNS COLDER
AND THIS PORK DISH IS CERTAINLY WARM, FILLING AND SUSTAINING.

Heat the oil in the open cooker and sauté the onion and garlic for 2 minutes. Add the pork and continue to sauté until the pork is completely sealed. Add the red and green peppers and sprinkle in the paprika. Sauté for 2 minutes before adding the contents of the can of tomatoes, a little salt and 150 ml/¼ pint of the stock. Close the lid and bring to 6.8-kg/15-lb pressure. Cook for 8 minutes then depressurize quickly and remove the lid. Stir in the aubergine.

Place the trivet rim-side down on top of the pork and line the separator with foil. Place the noodles into the separator and pour over the remaining stock. Place on the trivet. Close the lid and return to 6.8-kg/15-lb pressure. Cook for 5 minutes then depressurize quickly.

Remove the separator and drain the pasta noodles if necessary and place on a warmed serving platter.

Adjust the seasoning of the pork and stir the soured cream and chopped parsley into the cooked meat. Spoon on top of the cooked pasta and serve.

Serves **6**
Cook control **6.8 kg/15 lb**
Preparation time **10 minutes**
Open cooking time **7 minutes**
Pressure cooking time **13 minutes**

2 Tbsp oil
1 large onion, peeled and sliced
3 to 4 garlic cloves, peeled and crushed
675 g/1½ lb pork cubes
1 red pepper, seeded and cut into half moons

1 green pepper, seeded and cut into half moons
1 Tbsp paprika
One 400-g/14-oz can chopped tomatoes
Salt
600 ml/1 pt pork or vegetable stock
1 small aubergine, about 225 g/8 oz, trimmed and diced
225 g/8 oz pasta noodles
150 ml/¼ pt soured cream
2 Tbsp chopped fresh parsley

BOSTON BAKED BEANS WITH PORK

THE BENEFITS OF USING A PRESSURE COOKER CAN BE SEEN CLEARLY IN THIS DISH, WHICH WOULD NORMALLY TAKE 3 TO 4 HOURS TO COOK. THE COOKING TIME IS DRASTICALLY REDUCED, WITHOUT AFFECTING THE FLAVOUR.

Serves **4**
Cook control **6.8 kg/15 lb**
Preparation time **10 minutes plus 1 hour soaking**
Open cooking time **5 minutes**
Pressure cooking time **18 minutes**

225 g/8 oz dried haricot beans
1 Tbsp oil
2 medium onions, peeled and chopped
4 garlic cloves, peeled and chopped
450 g/1 lb pork belly, diced
1 tsp mustard powder
½ tsp ground cinnamon
¼ tsp ground cloves
1 Tbsp black treacle
1 Tbsp red wine vinegar
2 Tbsp tomato purée
One 400-g/14-oz can chopped tomatoes
250 ml/8 fl oz vegetable or chicken stock
Salt and freshly ground black pepper

TO GARNISH
2 Tbsp chopped fresh parsley and parsley sprigs

Cover the beans with boiling water and soak for 1 hour. Drain and set aside.

Heat the oil in the open cooker and sauté the onions, garlic and diced pork for 5 minutes. Blend the mustard and spices with the black treacle, vinegar and tomato purée and pour into the cooker. Add the beans with the chopped tomatoes and their juice, the stock and seasoning.

Close the lid and bring to 6.8-kg/15-lb pressure. Cook for 18 minutes.

Depressurize slowly then stir in the chopped parsley and serve garnished with parsley sprigs.

LAMB WITH PINTO BEANS

THIS RECIPE PROVIDES A WONDERFUL WARMING MEAL THAT IS JUST RIGHT FOR WHEN THE DAYS ARE BECOMING A LITTLE CHILLY. FOR EXTRA HEAT SIMPLY ADD A CHOPPED CHILLI OR TWO TO THE ONION, GARLIC AND FENNEL AT THE BEGINNING OF THE RECIPE.

Serves **4**
Cook control **6.8 kg/15 lb**
Preparation time **8 minutes plus 1 hour soaking time**
Open cooking time **6 minutes**
Pressure cooking time **12 minutes**

225 g/8 oz dried pinto beans
1 Tbsp oil
4 double loin lamb chops
1 medium onion, peeled and cut into wedges
4 garlic cloves, peeled and sliced
1 head fennel, trimmed and sliced
One 400-g/14-oz can chopped tomatoes
2 to 3 tsp Worcestershire sauce
1 Tbsp paprika
1 Tbsp tomato purée
300 ml/½ pt beef stock
Salt
2 Tbsp chopped fresh parsley

TO SERVE
Crusty bread and green salad

Cover the beans with boiling water and soak for 1 hour. Drain and set aside.

Heat the oil in the open cooker and brown the lamb chops on all sides. Remove from the cooker and set aside.

Add the onion, garlic and fennel to the cooker and sauté for 3 minutes then stir in the drained beans, the contents of the can of chopped tomatoes, the Worcestershire sauce and paprika.

Blend the tomato purée with the stock and stir into the bean mixture, place the lamb chops on top and bring to the boil. Close the lid, bring to 6.8-kg/15-lb pressure and cook for 12 minutes.

Depressurize slowly then remove the lamb chops. Add salt to taste to the bean mixture, then stir in the chopped parsley and serve the lamb chops with the beans, crusty bread and a green salad.

SPICED BEEF POT ROAST

THIS JOINT IS DELICIOUS WHETHER IT IS SERVED HOT OR COLD. WHEN COLD, IT MAKES AN IDEAL DISH TO SERVE FOR BUFFETS, PICNICS OR WITH SALAD WHEN DINING AL FRESCO.

Heat the oil in the open cooker and brown the joint on all sides. Remove from the cooker. Add the vegetables to the cooker and sauté for 5 minutes then remove with a slotted spoon and drain off any excess oil from the pan.

Add the stock and the wine and water mixture, stirring well to loosen any residue sticking to the pan, then place the trivet rim-side down in the cooker and place the joint onto the trivet. Arrange the vegetables around the meat.

Sprinkle the spices into the pan with the sugar and close the lid. Bring to 6.8-kg/15-lb pressure and cook for 45 minutes.

Depressurize quickly then lift out the joint and vegetables and place on a warmed serving plate and keep warm. Sprinkle the vegetables with the parsley just before serving.

Meanwhile strain the liquor in the pan then bring to the boil. Blend the cornflour with 1 tablespoon water and stir into the boiling liquor. Cook, stirring for 2 to 3 minutes or until thickened. Serve with the joint and vegetables.

Serves **6**
Cook control **6.8 kg/15 lb**
Preparation time **15 minutes**
Open cooking time **10 minutes**
Pressure cooking time
 45 minutes

1 Tbsp oil
One 1.5-kg/3-lb brisket or similar pot roasting joint
2 turnips, peeled and cut into chunks
2 large carrots, peeled and cut into chunks
10 baby onions, peeled
3 celery sticks, trimmed and sliced into chunks
300 ml/½ pt beef stock
300 ml/½ pt red wine and water mixed
About 10 cloves
2 bay leaves
1 cinnamon stick, bruised
1 small piece root ginger, chopped
1 Tbsp light soft brown sugar
1 Tbsp chopped fresh parsley
1 Tbsp cornflour

LIVER WITH MARSALA

MARSALA WINE IS A FORTIFIED WINE USED IN THE ITALIAN DESSERT, ZABAGLIONE. HERE I HAVE USED IT WITH LIVER GIVING A DELICIOUS RICH AND LUSCIOUS SAUCE NEEDING PLENTY OF BREAD OR POTATOES TO MOP UP.

Cut the liver into thin strips, rinse and pat dry with absorbent kitchen paper. Heat 1 tablespoon of the oil in the open cooker and brown the liver on all sides. Remove from the cooker and rinse the cooker. Add the remaining oil then the onion and garlic to the cooker and sauté for 3 minutes. Add the stock, wine and redcurrant jelly then arrange the liver on top.

Place the trivet rim-side down into the cooker and place the potatoes on top. Close the lid and bring to 6.8-kg/15-lb pressure. Cook for 3 minutes. Depressurize quickly and remove the lid.

Put the broccoli into the separator, place on top of the potatoes, close the lid and return to 6.8-kg/15-lb pressure. Cook for 2 minutes then depressurize quickly.

Remove the vegetables and liver from the cooker, place in warm serving dishes and keep warm.

Blend the butter and flour together to form a paste and bring the liquid remaining in the cooker to the boil. Whisk small spoonfuls of the flour paste into the liquid and continue whisking until the sauce has thickened and is smooth. Add seasoning to taste then pour over the liver, garnish and serve with the cooked vegetables.

Serves **4**
Cook control **6.8 kg/15 lb**
Preparation time **10 minutes**
Open cooking time **5 minutes**
Pressure cooking time **5 minutes**

550 g/1¼ lb lamb's liver, trimmed
2 Tbsp oil
1 medium onion, peeled and sliced
2 garlic cloves, peeled and sliced
250 ml/8 fl oz lamb or vegetable stock
50 ml/2 fl oz Marsala wine
1 Tbsp redcurrant jelly
675 g/1½ lb potatoes, peeled and cut into chunks
350 g/12 oz broccoli florets
1 Tbsp softened butter
1 Tbsp white plain flour
Salt and freshly ground black pepper

TO GARNISH
Flat-leaf parsley sprigs

BEEF IN SOURED CREAM SAUCE

THERE ARE MANY TYPES OF CHILLI AVAILABLE; I HAVE SUGGESTED JALAPEÑO FOR THIS RECIPE BECAUSE THEY ARE EXTREMELY EASY TO FIND, BUT YOU CAN SUBSTITUTE SERRANO OR ANOTHER VARIETY IF YOU PREFER.

Trim the steak, cut it into thin strips, and set aside. Heat 1 tablespoon of the oil in the open cooker then sauté the onions, garlic and chilli for 3 minutes. Add the mushrooms and pepper strips and continue to sauté for a further 2 minutes. Remove the vegetables from the cooker using a slotted spoon and reserve.

Add the remaining oil to the cooker then add the beef strips to the open cooker and cook for 3 to 5 minutes or until sealed, then return the onions and mushrooms to the cooker.

Blend the mustard, tomato purée and stock together then pour into the cooker. Add a little seasoning and nutmeg then close the lid.

Bring to 6.8-kg/15-lb pressure and cook for 8 minutes. Depressurize quickly then adjust the seasoning. Stir in the soured cream and parsley, stir well and serve.

Serves **4**
Cook control **6.8 kg/15 lb**
Preparation time **10 minutes**
Open cooking time **8 minutes**
Pressure cooking time **8 minutes**

450 g/1 lb rump steak
2 Tbsp oil
2 red onions, peeled and cut
  into wedges
3 to 4 garlic cloves, peeled
  and crushed
1 small red jalapeño chilli, seeded
  and chopped

100 g/4 oz assorted wild
  mushrooms, wiped and sliced
  if large
1 red pepper, seeded
  and sliced
1 tsp dry mustard
1 Tbsp tomato purée
250 ml/8 fl oz beef stock
Salt and freshly ground black
  pepper
¼ tsp grated fresh nutmeg
4 Tbsp soured cream
1 Tbsp chopped fresh
  flat-leaf parsley

BEEF WITH CAPER DUMPLINGS

WHEN PLACING MEAT, FISH OR ANY OTHER FOODS ONTO THE TRIVET, IT IS A GOOD IDEA
TO OIL THE TRIVET LIGHTLY FIRST. YOU CAN ALSO PLACE THE FOOD ON A PIECE OF GREASEPROOF
PAPER, WHICH MAKES IT EASY TO REMOVE ONCE COOKED.

Heat the oil in the open cooker and brown the joint on all sides. Remove from the cooker and wipe the cooker clean. Place the trivet rim-side down in the cooker and place the joint on top then add the bay leaves and mixed herbs.

Pour in the stock, close the lid and bring to 6.8-kg/15-lb pressure. Cook for 30 minutes.

Meanwhile prepare the vegetables and set aside. Mix the self-raising flour and suet together and stir in the capers, parsley and seasoning to taste. Mix to a soft dough with 6 to 7 tablespoons cold water. Form into 8 small balls and reserve.

Depressurize the meat quickly, remove the lid and arrange the prepared vegetables around the joint, and close the lid.

Return to 6.8-kg/15-lb pressure and cook for 5 minutes. Depressurize quickly and remove the vegetables and meat. Place on warmed serving dishes and keep warm. Place the dumplings on the trivet and return the cooker to the heat. Close the lid, but do not bring to pressure, and cook for 10 minutes or until the dumplings are fluffy and done. Remove from the cooker and place with the meat and vegetables.

Blend the cornflour with 2 tablespoons of water then stir into the liquid remaining in the open cooker. Cook, stirring until the liquid thickens, then serve with the meat, vegetables and dumplings.

Serves **6**
Cook control **6.8 kg/15 lb**
Preparation time **15 minutes**
Open cooking time **18 minutes**
Pressure cooking time
 35 minutes

1 Tbsp oil
1.5 kg/3 lb rolled beef joint, such as topside
2 bay leaves
2 Tbsp chopped fresh mixed herbs
600 ml/1 pt hot stock
2 medium carrots, peeled and cut into chunks
175 g/6 oz turnips, peeled and cut into chunks
2 leeks, trimmed and sliced
225 g/8 oz parsnips, peeled and cut into chunks
300 g/10 oz potatoes, peeled and cut into chunks
175 g/6 oz self-raising flour
75 g/3 oz suet
2 Tbsp capers, drained and chopped
1 Tbsp chopped fresh parsley
Salt and freshly ground black pepper
1 Tbsp cornflour

STUFFED VINE LEAVES

WHEN USING VINE LEAVES THAT HAVE BEEN PRESERVED IN BRINE, IT IS
IMPORTANT TO SOAK THEM WELL IN ORDER TO REMOVE THE TASTE OF THE BRINE.

Cover the vine leaves in almost-boiling water, leave for 20 minutes, drain well, and pat dry with absorbent kitchen paper.

Heat the oil in the open cooker and sauté the shallots, garlic and minced lamb for 5 minutes or until the lamb is sealed. Remove from the cooker and drain off any excess oil then place in a bowl. Wipe the base of the cooker clean.

Add the apricots, raisins, one tablespoon of orange zest, seasoning to taste and the chopped coriander. Mix well.

Place 2 to 3 vine leaves on a chopping board and place a spoonful of the lamb mixture on top. Roll up, encasing the mixture, and secure with fine twine. Repeat until all the vine leaves and minced lamb mixture have been used.

Blend the tomato purée with 300 ml/½ pint of the stock and pour into the cooker. Place the trivet into the cooker rim-side down and place the stuffed vine leaves on top.

Line the separator with foil. Mix the rice with the remaining orange zest and chopped red pepper and place into the foil-lined separator. Pour in the remaining stock and cover with foil. Secure firmly. Place on top of the vine leaves.

Close the lid and bring to 6.8-kg/15-lb pressure. Cook for 5 minutes. Depressurize quickly then arrange the rice in a warm serving platter, top with the vine leaves, garnish with coriander and serve.

Serves **4**
Cook control **6.8 kg/15 lb**
Preparation time **15 minutes**
  plus 20 minutes soaking
Open cooking time **5 minutes**
Pressure cooking time **5 minutes**

One pack preserved vine leaves
  (about 20)
1 Tbsp oil
3 shallots, peeled and finely
  chopped
2 garlic cloves, peeled and crushed
300 g/10 oz minced lamb
50 g/2 oz dried apricots, chopped
50 g/2 oz raisins
2 Tbsp grated orange zest

Salt and freshly ground
  black pepper
1 Tbsp chopped fresh coriander
1 Tbsp tomato purée
750 ml/1¼ pt lamb or vegetable
  stock
225 g/8 oz long-grain rice
1 red pepper, seeded
  and chopped

TO GARNISH
Fresh coriander sprigs

FARMHOUSE PÂTÉ

A CERTAIN AMOUNT OF LIQUID WILL OOZE OUT OF THE PÂTÉ AFTER IT IS DONE BUT
THIS WILL FLOW BACK INTO THE MEAT ON COOLING AND ENSURE THAT IT REMAINS MOIST.

Serves **8**
Cook control **6.8 kg/15 lb**
Preparation time **25 minutes plus overnight**
  chilling time
Pressure cooking time
  25 minutes

225 g/8 oz streaky bacon, derinded
4 shallots, peeled and chopped
4 garlic cloves, peeled and crushed
100 g/4 oz lamb's liver, chopped
225 g/8 oz minced pork
100 g/4 oz sausagemeat
2 Tbsp chopped fresh mixed herbs
Salt and freshly ground black pepper
¼ tsp freshly grated nutmeg
2 Tbsp brandy
1 Tbsp lemon juice

TO SERVE
Salad and crusty bread

Line a 750-ml/1¼-pint ovenproof dish with some bacon rashers, reserving the remainder. Mix the shallots, garlic, chopped liver, minced pork and sausagemeat until blended. Add the mixed herbs, seasoning and nutmeg, then stir in the brandy. Spoon the mixture into the bacon-lined dish and arrange the remaining bacon on top. Cover with a double layer of greaseproof paper and secure.

Place the trivet rim-side down in the cooker and add 450 ml/¾ pint water with the lemon juice. Stand the dish on the trivet, close the lid and bring to 6.8-kg/15-lb pressure. Cook for 25 minutes, depressurize quickly then take it out. Cover with greaseproof paper, cool then leave overnight in the refrigerator pressed down with a weight. Invert onto a serving plate and serve.

GINGER AND ORANGE GAMMON

A MOIST AND SUCCULENT PIECE OF GAMMON IS PERFECT TO SERVE FOR A DINNER PARTY OR FAMILY GET-TOGETHER.

Serves **6 to 8**
Cook control **6.8 kg/15 lb**
Preparation time **10 minutes**
Open cooking time **10 minutes plus**
  5 minutes standing time
Pressure cooking time
  24 minutes plus 15 minutes
  in oven

One 1.5-kg/3-lb gammon joint
One 7.5-cm/3-in piece root ginger, sliced
1 onion, peeled and cut into quarters
1 carrot, peeled and cut into chunks
About 26 cloves

Pared zest of 1 orange
3 Tbsp demerara sugar
1 tsp ground ginger
300 ml/½ pt orange juice
2 Tbsp soy sauce
1 Tbsp cornflour
2 tsp grated orange zest
Freshly ground black pepper

TO GARNISH
Orange wedges and parsley sprigs

TO SERVE
Freshly cooked vegetables

Place the joint in the open cooker and pour in sufficient water to half-fill, then add the sliced ginger, onion, carrot, about 6 of the whole cloves and the orange zest. Close the lid and bring to 6.8-kg/15-lb pressure.

Cook for 24 minutes, depressurize quickly and remove the meat. Reserve 150 ml/¼ pint of the cooking liquid. Allow to cool a little, strip off the skin and score the fat into a diamond pattern. Stud the scored fat with cloves.

Preheat the oven to 200°C/400°F/Gas 6. Place the meat in a roasting tin. Mix the sugar and ground ginger together and press onto the scored fat. Pour over the orange juice, the reserved cooking liquid and the soy sauce. Bake for 15 minutes or until the top is crisp, basting the joint occasionally with the juices in the pan. When done, remove the joint from the pan and keep warm.

Pour the juices into a saucepan and bring to the boil. Blend the cornflour with 1 tablespoon water and stir into the boiling liquid. Stir until slightly thickened. Add the orange zest with seasoning to taste then serve with the meat, garnished with orange and parsley and cooked vegetables.

BEEF OLIVES

IF YOU DO NOT HAVE A MEAT MALLET, A ROLLING PIN WORKS JUST AS WELL. PLACE THE STEAKS
BETWEEN 2 SHEETS OF GREASEPROOF PAPER SO THEY DO NOT TEAR WHILE BEING POUNDED.

Place the steaks between 2 sheets of greaseproof paper
and pound with a meat mallet until about 6 mm/¹/₄ inch thin.
Set aside.

Heat 1 tablespoon of the oil in the open cooker and sauté
the shallots and garlic for 3 minutes. Add the mushrooms
and continue to sauté for 2 minutes or until the mushrooms
have wilted. Remove from the heat and stir in the breadcrumbs,
orange zest, thyme and pine kernels with seasoning to taste.
Stir in the beaten egg and mix to a stiff consistency. Divide
between the four pieces of steak and roll up and secure with
fine twine.

Wipe the cooker clean, heat the remaining oil and brown
the beef rolls on all sides. Remove and drain off any excess
oil then replace the beef rolls and pour in the red wine and
150 ml/¹/₄ pint of the water.

Close the lid and bring to 6.8-kg/15-lb pressure. Cook for
15 minutes. Depressurize quickly and place the beef rolls onto
a warmed serving dish. Keep warm.

Blend the butter and flour together to form a paste. Add the
remaining water to the liquid in the cooker, bring to the boil
and whisk small spoonfuls of the paste into the boiling liquid.
Cook, still whisking, until a smooth, glossy and slightly
thickened sauce is formed. Add the red wine jelly or
redcurrant jelly to the sauce, adjust the seasoning and serve
with the garnished beef olives and freshly cooked vegetables.

Serves **4**
Cook control **6.8 kg/15 lb**
Preparation time **15 minutes**
Open cooking time **10 minutes**
Pressure cooking time
   15 minutes

**4 thin slices steak, such as topside
  or rump**
2 Tbsp oil
3 shallots, peeled and chopped
**2 garlic cloves, peeled
  and crushed**
**75 g/3 oz mushrooms, wiped and
  chopped**
50 g/2 ox fresh white breadcrumbs
1 Tbsp grated orange zest

1 Tbsp chopped fresh thyme
3 Tbsp pine kernels
**Salt and freshly ground
  black pepper**
1 small egg, beaten
300 ml/¹/₂ pt red wine
300 ml/¹/₂ pt water
1 Tbsp softened butter
1 Tbsp white plain flour
**3 to 4 tsp red wine jelly or red
  currant jelly**

TO GARNISH
Orange zest

TO SERVE
Freshly cooked vegetables

LAMB WITH AUBERGINE

BULGHUR WHEAT, ALSO KNOWN AS CRACKED WHEAT, IS A PROCESSED WHEAT POPULAR THROUGHOUT THE MIDDLE EAST. IT IS MOST COMMONLY USED IN TABBOULEH, A LEBANESE SALAD.

Trim the lamb, dice finely and set aside. Heat 1 tablespoon of the oil in the open cooker and sauté the lamb for 5 minutes or until sealed. Remove the lamb from the pan using a slotted spoon and set aside.

Add the remaining oil to the cooker then add the onions, garlic, aubergine and orange pepper and sauté for 1 minute.

Return the lamb to the cooker with the chopped tomatoes and their juice, and the stock, and add seasoning to taste. Close the lid and bring to 6.8-kg/15-lb pressure and cook for 10 minutes.

Meanwhile line the separator with foil and add the bulghur wheat mixed with the raisins, pine kernels and lemon zest. Pour in 450 ml/³⁄₄ pint of water, cover with greaseproof paper and secure.

Quickly depressurize the cooker, place the separator on top of the lamb then close the lid and return to pressure. Cook for 5 minutes.

Slowly depressurize the cooker and remove the bulghur wheat and lamb. Fluff up the bulghur wheat with a fork and spoon onto a warmed serving dish together with the cooked lamb. Sprinkle with the chopped coriander and serve.

Serves **4**
Cook control **6.8 kg/15 lb**
Preparation time **10 minutes**
Open cooking time **6 minutes**
Pressure cooking time **15 minutes**

450 g/1 lb lamb fillet
2 Tbsp oil
2 medium onions, peeled and cut into wedges
4 garlic cloves, peeled and chopped
1 aubergine, trimmed and cubed
1 orange pepper, seeded and chopped
One 400-g/14-oz can chopped tomatoes
150 ml/¼ pt lamb or vegetable stock
Salt and freshly ground black pepper
100 g/4 oz bulghur wheat
50 g/2 oz raisins
3 Tbsp pine kernels
1 Tbsp grated lemon zest

TO GARNISH
2 Tbsp chopped fresh coriander

ITALIAN LAMB WITH PASTA

ORIGINALLY GROWN IN EUROPE, FENNEL IS A BULBOUS LEAF STALK OFTEN REFERRED
TO AS FLORENCE FENNEL. IT CAN BE EATEN RAW OR COOKED AND HAS A TASTE SIMILAR TO ANISE.

Cover the dried mushrooms in almost boiling water
for 20 minutes, then drain, reserving the soaking liquor.

Heat 1 tablespoon of the oil in the open cooker and brown
the lamb shanks on all sides (this can be done in batches).
Remove from the cooker and add the remaining oil. Sauté
the garlic, sundried tomatoes, onion, fennel and all the
mushrooms for 5 minutes or until the onion has softened.
Remove from the cooker and set aside. Pour in the passata
and red wine and stir well to remove any sediment sticking to
the base.

Place the trivet rim-side down into the cooker and place
the lamb shanks on top. Arrange the onion and mushroom
mixture over the lamb and add the chopped oregano and
seasoning to taste. Close the lid and bring to 6.8-kg/15-lb
pressure and cook for 20 minutes.

Depressurize quickly and remove the lid. Remove the lamb
and vegetables and keep warm. Place the pasta in the
foil-lined separator with 600 ml/1 pint boiling water, cover
with foil and secure with fine twine. Place on the trivet.
Close the lid and return to pressure. Cook for 5 minutes
then depressurize quickly.

Drain the pasta and serve with the lamb, vegetables
and sauce on a warmed serving platter, garnished with
fresh oregano sprigs.

Serves **4**
Cook control **6.8 kg/15 lb**
Preparation time **10 minutes**
Open cooking time **10 minutes**
Pressure cooking time
  25 minutes

15 g/½ oz dried mushrooms
2 Tbsp oil
Two 225-g/8-oz lamb shanks
4 garlic cloves, peeled
  and crushed
25 g/1 oz sundried tomatoes,
  chopped

1 medium onion, peeled and cut
  into wedges
1 head fennel, trimmed and sliced
100 g/4 oz button mushrooms,
  wiped
300 ml/½ pt passata
300 ml/½ pt red wine
1 Tbsp chopped fresh oregano
Salt and freshly ground
  black pepper
225 g/8 oz dried pasta shapes

TO GARNISH
Fresh oregano sprigs

HERB MEAT LOAF

YOU CAN USE MINCED BEEF, LAMB, PORK OR CHICKEN FOR THIS DISH, BUT BUY THE BEST QUALITY YOU CAN AFFORD. CHEAPER MINCED MEAT CONTAINS A LOT OF FAT AND YOU WILL END UP WITH A MUCH SMALLER LOAF.

Place the minced beef, sausagemeat, onion, garlic, herbs and breadcrumbs into a mixing bowl and mix well. Blend the tomato purée and horseradish sauce with seasoning and add to the mixture, then add the egg and sufficient brandy to bind the mixture together.

Place in a 900-ml/1½ pint ovenproof container and press down lightly. Cover with a double layer of greaseproof paper.

Place the trivet in the cooker rim-side down and add 600 ml/ 1 pint water and 2 tablespoons lemon juice. Place the container on top of the trivet and close the lid. Bring to 6.8-kg/15-lb pressure and cook for 20 minutes. Depressurize quickly, remove the greaseproof paper and serve immediately, garnished with herbs, with gravy and freshly cooked vegetables.

Serves **8**
Cook control **6.8 kg/15 lb**
Preparation time **10 minutes**
Pressure cooking time
20 minutes

450 g/1 lb minced beef
100 g/4 oz sausagemeat
1 medium onion, peeled and
    finely chopped
2 garlic cloves, peeled
    and crushed
2 Tbsp chopped fresh mixed herbs
50 g/2 oz fresh white breadcrumbs

2 Tbsp tomato purée
1 Tbsp hot horseradish sauce
Salt and freshly ground
    black pepper
1 medium egg
2 to 3 Tbsp brandy
2 Tbsp lemon juice

TO GARNISH
Fresh herb sprigs

TO SERVE
Gravy and freshly cooked
    vegetables

POULTRY

CHICKEN CHASSEUR

IF A WINE IS NOT WORTH DRINKING, IT IS RARELY WORTH USING IT FOR COOKING.
TRY TO USE GOOD WINE FOR COOKING, OR YOU MAY SPOIL THE FINISHED DISH.

Heat the oil in the open cooker and sauté the onions and bacon until lightly browned. Remove. Seal the chicken portions on all sides in the oil remaining in the cooker then remove from the cooker and drain off any excess oil.

Return the onions, bacon and chicken to the pan and add the mushrooms and tomatoes. Blend the tomato purée with the wine and stock then pour over the chicken. Close the lid and bring to 6.8-kg/15-lb pressure and cook for 5 minutes.

Depressurize quickly, lift out the chicken and vegetables and keep warm. Blend the flour and butter together to form a paste. Bring the liquid in the pan to the boil then whisk small amounts of the flour paste into the boiling liquid. Cook until smooth and thickened. Add seasoning to taste then pour the sauce over the chicken and onions, sprinkle with parsley and serve with mashed potatoes and either a green salad or freshly cooked vegetables.

Serves **4**
Cook control **6.8 kg/15 lb**
Preparation time **12 minutes**
Open cooking time **5 minutes**
Pressure cooking time **5 minutes**

2 Tbsp oil
8 baby onions, peeled
50 g/2 oz chopped streaky bacon
4 boneless, skinless chicken portions
225 g/8 oz large field mushrooms, wiped and sliced
8 cherry tomatoes, halved

2 Tbsp tomato purée
300ml/½ pt red wine
150 ml/¼ pt chicken stock
1 Tbsp white plain flour
1 Tbsp softened butter
Salt and freshly ground black pepper

TO GARNISH
1 Tbsp chopped fresh parsley

TO SERVE
Mashed potatoes, and green salad or vegetables

COQ AU VIN

THIS CLASSIC FRENCH DISH WORKS PERFECTLY WHEN COOKED IN THE PRESSURE COOKER. FOR A MORE INTENSE FLAVOUR, MARINATE THE CHICKEN PORTIONS IN THE RED WINE AND BRANDY FOR 2 TO 3 HOURS BEFORE COOKING.

Heat the oil in the open cooker and brown the chicken portions on all sides. Remove from the cooker and reserve. Add the shallots, garlic and bacon to the cooker and sauté for 3 minutes then add the mushrooms and continue to sauté for 1 minute.

Return the chicken portions to the cooker and pour in the red wine, stock and seasoning to taste.

Close the lid and bring to 6.8-kg/15-lb pressure and cook for 5 minutes. Depressurize quickly and remove the lid. Pour over the brandy and stir.

Place the trivet in the cooker rim-side down. Place the potatoes in the separator and place on top of the trivet and close the lid.

Return to 6.8-kg/15-lb pressure and cook for 4 minutes then depressurize quickly. Remove the lid and separator, place the potatoes in a serving dish and keep warm. Remove the chicken from the cooker with the shallots and mushrooms, place on a warmed serving dish and keep warm.

Blend the butter and flour together to form a smooth paste then bring the liquid in the cooker to the boil and whisk in small spoonfuls of the paste. Continue to whisk until the sauce is smooth and thickened. Adjust seasoning to taste, stir in the crème fraîche or soured cream with the parsley, pour over the chicken and shallots and serve.

Serves **4**
Cook control **6.8 kg/15 lb**
Preparation time **10 minutes**
Open cooking time **10 minutes**
Pressure cooking time **9 minutes**

1 Tbsp oil
Four 175-g/6-oz chicken quarters
8 shallots, peeled
**4 to 6 garlic cloves, peeled and
   sliced**
8 rashers bacon, cut into small dice
100 g/4 oz button mushrooms, wiped
300 ml/½ pt red wine
150 ml/¼ pt chicken broth
**Salt and freshly ground
   black pepper**
3 Tbsp brandy
350 g/12 oz baby new potatoes
1 Tbsp softened butter
1 Tbsp white plain flour
**2 Tbsp crème fraîche or soured
   cream**
1 Tbsp chopped fresh parsley

ALMOND AND PECAN-STUFFED
CHICKEN BREASTS

THIS DELICIOUS RECIPE COMBINES THE CLASSIC FLAVOURS OF CITRUS AND FRESH HERBS WITH CHICKEN AND NUTS FOR A HEALTHY YET FILLING DISH.

Wipe the chicken breasts and, using a sharp knife, slit along the longest edge of each chicken breast to form a pocket. Wipe with absorbent kitchen paper and set aside.

Mix together the spring onions, ground almonds, breadcrumbs, pecans, lemon zest, tarragon and seasoning and bind together with the beaten egg and sufficient orange juice to make a moist but not wet stuffing. Use to stuff the cavities in the chicken breasts. Press the edges firmly together.

Melt the butter with the oil in the open cooker then brown the chicken on all sides. Pour in the remaining orange juice with the honey and close the lid. Bring to 6.8-kg/15-lb pressure and cook for 5 minutes. Depressurize quickly then lift out the chicken and keep warm. Strain the cooking juices into a cleaned pan and bring to the boil. Blend the cornflour with 1 tablespoon water and add to the boiling liquor. Cook, stirring until slightly thickened. Pour over the chicken and garnish with the tarragon sprigs and orange wedges. Serve with green salad or freshly cooked vegetables and new potatoes or noodles.

Serves **4**
Cook control **6.8 kg/15 lb**
Preparation time **10 minutes**
Open cooking time **5 minutes**
Pressure cooking time **5 minutes**

4 boneless, skinless chicken breasts
6 spring onions, trimmed and chopped
50 g/2 oz ground almonds
25 g/1 oz fresh white breadcrumbs
50 g/2 oz pecans, chopped
1 Tbsp grated lemon zest
1 Tbsp chopped fresh tarragon
Salt and freshly ground black pepper

1 medium egg, beaten
300 ml/½ pt orange juice
1 Tbsp butter
1 Tbsp oil
2 tsp honey
1 Tbsp cornflour

TO GARNISH
Fresh tarragon sprigs and orange wedges

TO SERVE
Green salad or freshly cooked vegetables, and new potatoes or noodles

TURKEY WITH TARRAGON

TARRAGON IS A HERB THAT GOES PARTICULARLY WELL WITH BOTH POULTRY AND FISH.

Serves **4**
Cook control **6.8 kg/15 lb**
Preparation time **5 minutes**
Open cooking time
   5 to 6 minutes
Pressure cooking time
   7 minutes

2 Tbsp oil
450 g/1 lb boneless, skinless
   turkey thigh, diced
2 medium onions, peeled
   and sliced
1 head fennel, trimmed
   and sliced
2 large carrots, peeled and
   cut into half moons

150 ml/¼ pt dry white wine
300 ml/½ pt turkey or chicken
   stock
2 Tbsp chopped fresh tarragon
1 Tbsp grated orange zest
Salt and freshly ground
   black pepper
1 Tbsp cornflour

TO GARNISH

Orange zest, orange wedges
   and tarragon sprigs

TO SERVE

New potatoes, mangetout and
   broccoli

Heat 1 tablespoon of the oil in the open cooker and seal the diced turkey on all sides. Using a slotted spoon remove the turkey from the cooker and reserve. Add the remaining oil to the cooker and sauté the onion, fennel and carrot for 5 minutes.

Return the turkey to the cooker then add the wine, stock, tarragon and orange zest with seasoning to taste. Close the lid, bring to 6.8-kg/15-lb pressure. Cook for 7 minutes and depressurize quickly. Remove the turkey and vegetables from the cooker with a slotted spoon and keep warm.

Bring the liquor remaining in the cooker to the boil. Blend the cornflour with 1 tablespoon water, stir into the boiling liquid and cook, stirring until thickened. Adjust the seasoning, pour the sauce over the turkey, garnish and serve.

CORIANDER CHICKEN

THIS DISH OFFERS A SPICY FLAVOUR, WHICH IS TEMPERED BY THE SMOOTH COCONUT MILK.

Serves **4**
Cook control **6.8 kg/15 lb**
Preparation time **10 minutes**
Open cooking time **8 minutes**
Pressure cooking time
   10 minutes

2 Tbsp oil
Four 225-g/8-oz chicken
   portions, thoroughly defrosted
   if frozen
1 medium onion, peeled and
   cut into wedges
4 garlic cloves, peeled and
   chopped

1 Tbsp mild curry paste
4 medium tomatoes, skinned,
   seeded and chopped
300 ml/½ pt coconut milk
150 ml/¼ pt chicken stock
300 g/10 oz sweet potatoes,
   peeled and diced
1 green pepper, seeded and
   chopped
225 g/8 oz green beans, trimmed
   and halved
Salt
1 tsp paprika
1 Tbsp cornflour
2 Tbsp chopped fresh coriander

Heat 1 tablespoon of the oil in the open cooker and brown the chicken portions on all sides. Remove from the cooker and set aside. Add the remaining oil then the onion and garlic to the cooker and sauté for 1 minute, then add the curry paste and cook, stirring for 2 minutes. Add the chopped tomatoes, coconut milk, stock, diced sweet potato and the reserved chicken and close the lid. Bring to 6.8-kg/15-lb pressure and cook for 8 minutes then depressurize quickly.

Remove the lid and add the green pepper and beans, close the lid, and return to 6.8-kg/15-lb pressure. Cook for 2 minutes then depressurize quickly and remove the chicken portions.

Add salt and paprika to taste then blend the cornflour with 1 tablespoon of water and stir into the cooker. Cook, stirring until the sauce thickens, then stir in the chopped coriander, pour over the chicken and serve.

CHICKEN WITH OKRA
AND FENNEL TAGINE

OKRA, ALSO KNOWN AS LADIES' FINGERS, IS AN ANNUAL PLANT OF THE COTTON FAMILY AND NATIVE TO AFRICA. WELL KNOWN IN CREOLE COOKING, IT IS USED WHEN MAKING GUMBO.

Heat 1 tablespoon of the oil in the open cooker and sauté the chicken for 5 minutes until well-sealed and golden brown. Using a slotted spoon, remove from the cooker and reserve.

Add the remaining oil to the cooker and sauté the onion, garlic, ginger, chilli and fennel for 2 minutes. Return the chicken to the cooker with the saffron, tomatoes, courgette, okra, apricots and cinnamon sticks.

Pour in the stock, add seasoning to taste, then close the lid and bring to 6.8-kg/15-lb pressure. Cook for 3 minutes then depressurize quickly. Discard the cinnamon sticks and serve garnished with the olives and parsley and either freshly cooked cinnamon-flavoured bulghur wheat, couscous or potatoes, and salad.

Serves **4**
Cook control **6.8 kg/15 lb**
Preparation time **15 minutes**
Open cooking time **8 minutes**
Pressure cooking time **3 minutes**

2 Tbsp oil
450 g/1 lb diced fresh boneless, skinless chicken
1 medium onion, peeled and sliced
3 garlic cloves, peeled and sliced
1 small piece root ginger, peeled and grated
1 small jalapeño chilli, seeded and chopped
1 head fennel, trimmed and chopped
A few strands saffron
3 medium tomatoes, seeded and chopped
1 large courgette, trimmed and chopped
225 g/8 oz okra, trimmed and chopped in half if large
75 g/3 oz dried apricots, chopped
2 cinnamon sticks, bruised
300 ml/½ pt chicken stock
Salt and freshly ground black pepper

TO GARNISH
A few black olives and flat-leaf parsley

TO SERVE
Cinnamon-flavoured bulghur wheat, couscous or potatoes, and salad

POUSSINS
WITH KUMQUATS

KUMQUATS ARE TINY, SLIGHTLY BITTER-TASTING ORANGES WHICH ARE EATEN WHOLE. IF PREFERRED
SUBSTITUTE WITH 1 TO 2 ORDINARY ORANGES OR, IF AVAILABLE, BLOOD ORANGES.

Halve the poussins, rinse and pat dry. Heat the oil in the open cooker and seal the poussins on all sides. Remove from the cooker and wipe the cooker clean.

Return the poussins to the cooker with the unpeeled garlic cloves, bay leaves, stock and orange juice. Sprinkle in the orange zest, vinegar and sugar with the soy sauce and add the tarragon with a little seasoning. Cut the kumquats in half, add to the cooker and close the lid.

Bring to 6.8-kg/15-lb pressure and cook for 10 minutes. Depressurize quickly then remove the poussins and kumquats from the cooker and place on a warmed serving plate. Strain the liquid, return to the cooker and bring to the boil. Blend the cornflour with 1 tablespoon water and stir into the boiling liquid. Cook, stirring until the sauce thickens. Adjust the seasoning, garnish the poussins and serve with the sauce and freshly cooked vegetables.

Serves **4**
Cook control **6.8 kg/15 lb**
Preparation time **5 minutes**
Open cooking time **5 minutes**
Pressure cooking time
   10 minutes

2 large poussins
2 Tbsp oil
10 unpeeled garlic cloves
2 bay leaves
300 ml/½ pt chicken stock
150 ml/¼ pt orange juice
1 Tbsp grated orange zest
2 Tbsp white wine vinegar
1 Tbsp light soft brown sugar
2 Tbsp dark soy sauce
1 Tbsp chopped fresh tarragon
Salt and freshly ground black
   pepper
12 kumquats
1 Tbsp cornflour

TO GARNISH
Fresh tarragon sprigs and extra
   kumquats

TO SERVE
Freshly cooked vegetables

CAJUN TURKEY

TURKEY HAS THE LOWEST FAT CONTENT OF ALL MEAT AND POULTRY AND IS THEREFORE IDEAL FOR PEOPLE WHO ARE WATCHING THEIR CALORIE INTAKE. ANOTHER BONUS IS THAT IT COMBINES WELL WITH MANY DIVERSE FLAVOURS.

Trim the turkey, dice, place in a shallow dish then scatter over the chopped onion, garlic, dried crushed chillies and cardamom pods. Blend the spices and lemon zest with the golden syrup, ketchup and lemon juice, mix well then pour over the turkey. Cover loosely and allow to marinate in the refrigerator for at least 30 minutes, overnight if time permits. Stir the turkey occasionally during this time.

When ready to cook, heat the oil in the open cooker, drain the turkey and seal the turkey on all sides. Stir half the marinade into 300 ml/½ pint of the stock then pour over the turkey.

Place the trivet rim-side down on top of the turkey and line the separator with foil. Place the pasta into the separator and pour over the remaining stock. Cover with a double sheet of greaseproof paper.

Close the lid and bring to 6.8-kg/15-lb pressure and cook for 5 minutes. Depressurize quickly then remove the pasta and drain if necessary.

Blend the cornflour with 1 tablespoon water and stir into the cooker. Bring to the boil and cook, stirring until the sauce has thickened. Stir the chopped coriander into the pasta and serve with the cooked turkey.

Serves **4**
Cook control **6.8 kg/15 lb**
Preparation time **15 minutes**
   plus 30 minutes marinating time
Open cooking time **3 minutes**
Pressure cooking time **5 minutes**

450 g/1 lb fresh turkey breast meat
1 medium onion, peeled and chopped
4 garlic cloves, peeled and crushed
½ to 1 tsp dried crushed chillies
5 cardamom pods, bruised
1 tsp ground coriander
½ tsp mixed spice
1 tsp paprika
1 Tbsp grated lemon zest
2 tsp golden syrup, warmed
4 Tbsp ketchup
2 Tbsp lemon juice
1 Tbsp oil
680 ml/1¼ pt turkey or chicken stock, hot
150 g/6 oz dried pasta shapes
1 Tbsp cornflour
2 Tbsp chopped fresh coriander

APRICOT AND CRANBERRY-
STUFFED TURKEY

SMALL TURKEY JOINTS MAKE AN EXCELLENT MEAL AND ARE QUICKLY COOKED
WHEN USING THE PRESSURE COOKER.

Wipe the turkey joint and make two deep pockets along each length of the joint. Set aside.

Heat 1 tablespoon of the oil in the open cooker and sauté the shallots, garlic and mushrooms for 5 minutes. Place into a bowl and wipe the cooker clean.

Add the apricots, cranberry sauce, orange zest, breadcrumbs, parsley and seasoning to taste to the shallots and mix to a stiff consistency with the egg and orange juice. Use to stuff the pockets in the turkey. Pinch the edges together and if liked bind with fine twine.

Heat the remaining oil in the cooker, seal the joint on all sides and then cover with the bacon. Pour in the stock and wine and add the redcurrant jelly. Close the lid and bring to 6.8-kg/15-lb pressure. Cook for 15 minutes. Depressurize quickly and remove the joint from the cooker. Keep warm.

Bring the liquor in the cooker to the boil and cook, stirring until the sauce thickens, then strain into a serving jug. Garnish the joint and serve with the sauce and freshly cooked vegetables.

Serves **4 to 6**
Cook control **6.8 kg/15 lb**
Preparation time **10 minutes**
Open cooking time **5 minutes**
Pressure cooking time
  15 minutes

1 whole turkey breast fillet joint
2 Tbsp oil
4 shallots, peeled and chopped
2 garlic cloves, peeled and
  crushed
75 g/3 oz button mushrooms,
  wiped and chopped
75 g/3 oz dried apricots, chopped
2 Tbsp cranberry sauce
1 Tbsp grated orange zest
75 g/3 oz fresh white breadcrumbs

2 Tbsp chopped fresh parsley
Salt and freshly ground black
  pepper
1 medium egg, beaten
1 to 2 Tbsp orange juice
8 to 10 rashers streaky bacon
150 ml/¼ pt turkey or chicken
  stock
300 ml/½ pt rosé or white wine
1 Tbsp redcurrant jelly

TO GARNISH
Fresh cranberries and fresh
  apricots

TO SERVE
Freshly cooked potatoes
  and vegetables

PHEASANT
WITH RED CABBAGE

THE RED CABBAGE AND APPLE ARE A PERFECT FOIL FOR THE PHEASANTS IN THIS DISH.

Wipe the pheasant joints then heat the oil in the open cooker and brown the joints on all sides (this takes about 5 minutes). Remove from the cooker and wipe the cooker clean.

Thoroughly rinse the red cabbage in cold water and drain well. Place in a bowl with the chopped onion, apple, sugar, dill and seasoning to taste. Mix well and pour over the balsamic vinegar.

Place the joints in the cooker and pour over the stock. Put the trivet in the cooker rim-side down and place the red cabbage on the trivet. Close the lid and bring to 6.8-kg/15-lb pressure. Cook for 10 minutes then depressurize quickly. Remove the joints and cabbage from the cooker and keep warm.

Blend the butter and flour together to form a paste. Bring the liquid remaining in the cooker to the boil then whisk in small spoonfuls of the flour paste. Continue to whisk until the sauce has thickened and is smooth. Serve with the pheasants, the red cabbage and mashed potatoes. Garnish with dill sprigs.

Serves **4**
Cook control **6.8 kg/15 lb**
Preparation time **15 minutes**
Open cooking time **5 minutes**
Pressure cooking time
  10 minutes

4 small or 2 large pheasants, jointed, or use guinea fowl
1 Tbsp oil
1 small red cabbage (about 675 g/1½ lb in weight) trimmed and shredded
1 onion, peeled and chopped
1 large cooking apple, peeled, cored and chopped
1 Tbsp dark soft brown sugar

2 Tbsp chopped fresh dill
Salt and freshly ground black pepper
1 Tbsp balsamic vinegar
300 ml/½ pt chicken stock
1 Tbsp softened butter
1 Tbsp white plain flour

TO GARNISH
Dill sprigs

TO SERVE
Mashed potatoes

PHEASANT WITH CANNELLINI BEANS AND OLIVES

THIS IS THE KIND OF DISH THAT APPEALS TO MEN, AS IT IS MEATY, FULL OF FLAVOUR AND THERE'S PLENTY OF IT!

Cover the beans in boiling water and soak for 1 hour. Drain and reserve. Cut the pheasants into joints, rinse and dry well on absorbent kitchen paper.

Heat 1 tablespoon of the oil and seal the joints all over then remove from the cooker and set aside. Add the remaining oil, onion and garlic and sauté for 3 minutes then add the mushrooms and continue to sauté for 1 minute.

Return the beans to the cooker and place the joints on top. Pour over the red wine and stock with the honey and add a little seasoning with all but 1 tablespoon of the olives.

Close the lid, bring to 6.8-kg/15-lb pressure and cook for 10 minutes.

Depressurize quickly and remove the joints from the cooker. Keep warm. Drain off the liquid from the beans, arrange the beans round the pheasant and return the liquid to the cooker.

Blend the butter and flour together to form a smooth paste. Bring the liquid in the cooker to a gentle boil then whisk in small spoonfuls of the flour paste. Cook, whisking until the sauce thickens and is smooth. Adjust the seasoning, add the remaining black olives and the chopped parsley and pour over the joints. Serve with mashed potatoes and freshly cooked green vegetables.

Serves **4**
Cook control **6.8 kg/15 lb**
Preparation time **10 minutes**
  plus 1 hour soaking time
Open cooking time **9 minutes**
Pressure cooking time
  10 minutes

225 g/8 oz dried cannellini beans
2 large pheasants (about
  1.25 kg/2½ lb total weight)
2 Tbsp oil
1 medium onion, peeled and sliced
3 garlic cloves, peeled and
  chopped

225 g/8 oz closed-cup
  mushrooms, wiped and chopped
150 ml/¼ pt red wine
300 ml/½ pt chicken stock
2 tsp honey
Salt and freshly ground black
  pepper
75 g/3 oz stoned black olives
1 Tbsp softened butter
1 Tbsp white plain flour
2 Tbsp chopped fresh parsley

TO SERVE
Mashed potatoes and freshly
  cooked green vegetables

CARIBBEAN CHICKEN

YAMS FEATURE PROMINENTLY IN WEST INDIAN COOKING AND ARE COOKED LIKE POTATOES.

Heat the oil in the open cooker and seal the chicken portions on all sides, remove from the cooker and reserve. Add the garlic, chilli and yam to the oil remaining in the cooker and sauté in the open cooker for 5 minutes or until soft. Add the sliced peppers and cook for 2 minutes. Remove all the vegetables from the pan and clean.

Return the chicken and yam mixture to the cooker with the chopped mango, brown sugar, juice, stock and soy sauce. Add seasoning, close the lid and bring to 6.8-kg/15-lb pressure. Cook for 10 minutes. Depressurize quickly then remove the chicken and yam, straining off the liquid, and place on a warm serving platter. Keep warm. Bring the cooking liquid to the boil in the open cooker and add the coriander. Blend the cornflour with 1 tablespoon water then stir into the boiling liquid. Cook, stirring until thickened. Adjust seasoning then pour over the chicken. Garnish and serve.

Serves **4**
Cook control **6.8 kg/15 lb**
Preparation time **10 minutes**
Open cooking time **12 minutes**
Pressure cooking time
 10 minutes

2 Tbsp oil
4 skinless chicken portions
4 garlic cloves, peeled and
 chopped in half
1 green serrano chilli, seeded
 and chopped
1 large yam, peeled and cubed
1 red pepper, seeded and sliced
1 yellow pepper, seeded
 and sliced
1 almost ripe mango, peeled,
 stoned and chopped
2 tsp soft brown sugar
150 ml/¼ pt mango or
 orange juice
300 ml/½ pt chicken stock
2 Tbsp dark soy sauce
Salt and freshly ground black
 pepper
2 Tbsp chopped fresh coriander
1 Tbsp cornflour

TO GARNISH
Extra chopped mango and
 coriander

SPICED CHICKEN WITH
CRANBERRIES AND ORANGE

THERE IS SOMETHING VERY EVOCATIVE ABOUT THE FRAGRANCE OF CRANBERRIES COOKING;
PERHAPS IT IS BECAUSE THEY ARE ASSOCIATED WITH CHILDHOOD AND CHRISTMAS.

Dice the chicken thighs then heat 1 tablespoon of the oil in the open cooker and seal the chicken on all sides. Using a slotted spoon remove the chicken from the cooker. Add the remaining oil to the cooker then sauté the shallots and celery for 5 minutes or until beginning to soften.

Return the chicken to the cooker then add the rosemary sprigs, cranberries, orange zest, cinnamon stick, orange juice and stock with seasoning. Close the lid and bring to 6.8-kg/15-lb pressure and cook for 3 minutes. Depressurize quickly then place the trivet on top.

Line the separator with foil and place the pasta in the separator with 600 ml/1 pint boiling water. Place on the trivet and close the lid. Return to pressure and cook for 5 minutes. Depressurize quickly, then remove the separator and drain the pasta. Serve the chicken on top of the pasta, garnished with the rosemary sprigs, cranberries and orange wedges.

Serves **4**
Cook control **6.8 kg/15 lb**
Preparation time **5 minutes**
Open cooking time **10 minutes**
Pressure cooking time **8 minutes**

8 skinless, boneless chicken thighs
2 Tbsp oil
8 shallots, peeled and cut into wedges
4 celery sticks, trimmed and cut into chunks
2 small sprigs fresh rosemary
100 g/4 oz fresh or defrosted frozen cranberries
1 long strip thin pared orange zest
1 cinnamon stick, bruised
4 Tbsp orange juice
150 ml/¼ pint chicken stock
Salt and freshly ground black pepper
225 g/8 oz pasta shapes

TO GARNISH
Rosemary sprigs, cranberries and orange wedges

DUCK WITH FIGS AND PORT

I PREFER TO EAT MY DUCK BREASTS SLIGHTLY PINK BUT IF YOU LIKE YOUR DUCK WELL DONE, JUST COOK FOR AN EXTRA 1 TO 2 MINUTES.

Wipe the duck breasts and make 3 diagonal slashes across each. Heat the oil in the open cooker then seal the duck breasts on all sides. Remove from the cooker with a slotted spoon and drain on absorbent kitchen paper.

Add the shallots to the oil remaining in the cooker and sauté for 3 minutes then drain off any excess oil and add the chopped dried figs.

Return the duck breasts to the cooker and pour in the orange juice, stock and port, seasoning to taste.

Close the lid and bring to 6.8-kg/15-lb pressure. Cook for 12 to 15 minutes (depending on whether you like your duck medium rare or well done). Depressurize quickly and remove the duck from the cooker and keep warm. Place the shallots and figs with the liquid into a blender and blend to form a purée. Return to the cooker, stir in the cream and heat gently. Adjust the seasoning then pour over the duck breasts and serve, garnished with fresh figs, with freshly cooked vegetables.

Serves **4**
Cook control **6.8 kg/15 lb**
Preparation time **5 minutes**
Open cooking time **8 minutes**
Pressure cooking time
   12 to 15 minutes

4 boneless duck breasts
1 Tbsp oil
4 shallots, peeled and cut
   into wedges
75 g/3 oz ready-to eat dried figs,
   chopped

150 ml/¼ pt orange juice
150 ml/¼ pt chicken stock
3 Tbsp port
Salt and freshly ground black
   pepper
4 Tbsp single cream

TO GARNISH
Fresh figs

TO SERVE
Freshly cooked vegetables

LEMON-BRAISED CHICKEN
WITH CUMIN

THIS CHICKEN DISH IS PERFECT FOR A SPRING DAY, WHEN YOU WANT A MORE SUBSTANTIAL MEAL THAN SALAD. THIS VERSION, USING SPRING ONION IN THE MASHED POTATOES, IS A REAL WINNER.

Cut the chicken into bite-sized pieces and reserve. Heat the oil in the open cooker and brown the chicken on all sides. Using a slotted spoon remove the chicken from the cooker and set aside.

Add the onion to the cooker and sauté for 2 minutes. Add the lemon, cumin seeds and ground coriander and sauté for 1 minute. Return the chicken to the cooker. Pour in the white wine, 150 ml/¼ pint water, the honey and a little seasoning.

Place the trivet rim-side down in the cooker and place the separator on top. Place the potatoes in the separator and close the lid. Bring to 6.8-kg/15-lb pressure and cook for 3 minutes.

Depressurize quickly then remove the potatoes from the cooker and place in a bowl. Add seasoning to taste with the butter, and mash until smooth. Add the cream or yoghurt with the spring onions and mix well. Keep warm.

Blend the cornflour with 2 tablespoons water and stir into the chicken and liquor left in the cooker. Cook over a gentle heat, stirring until thickened. Adjust the seasoning then serve with the spring onion-flavoured mashed potatoes and a green salad.

Serves **4**
Cook control **6.8 kg/15 lb**
Preparation time **10 minutes**
Open cooking time **8 minutes**
Pressure cooking time **3 minutes**

550 g/1¼ lb skinless boneless chicken
1 Tbsp oil
1 medium onion, peeled, sliced and cut into half-moon shapes
1 small lemon, sliced and cut into half-moon shapes
1 tsp cumin seeds
½ tsp ground coriander
150 ml/¼ pt medium dry white wine

2 tsp honey
Salt and freshly ground black pepper
675 g/1½ lb potatoes, peeled and cut into chunks
2 Tbsp butter
2 Tbsp single cream or low-fat, natural yoghurt
4 to 5 spring onions, trimmed and chopped
1 Tbsp cornflour

TO SERVE
Salad

BLACK-EYED BEAN
AND CHICKEN CASSEROLE

BONELESS CHICKEN THIGH MEAT WORKS VERY WELL IN THIS RECIPE. THE SLIGHTLY MORE GAMEY
FLAVOUR OF THE THIGH MEAT COMPLEMENTS THE BEANS.

Cover the dried beans with boiling water, soak for 1 hour then drain. Place the beans in the open cooker with 600 ml/1 pint cold water and bring to the boil. Remove any scum that floats to the surface then reduce the heat slightly. Close the lid and, maintaining the same heat, bring to 6.8-kg/15-lb pressure. Cook for 5 minutes then depressurize slowly.

Discard the cooking liquid and reserve the beans. Wipe the cooker clean, heat the oil in the open cooker and seal the gammon and chicken all over.

Add the onion, fennel and carrots and continue to cook for 3 minutes, stirring frequently.

Add the contents of the can of tomatoes and return the beans to the cooker. Add seasoning to taste, the Cajun seasoning, oregano and stock and stir lightly. Arrange the sliced sweet potatoes on top and close the lid.

Bring to 6.8-kg/15-lb pressure and cook for 5 minutes then depressurize slowly. Remove the lid and arrange the chicken, beans and sweet potatoes in a warm dish, sprinkle with the herbs and serve with crusty bread.

Serves **6**
Cook control **6.8 kg/15 lb**
Preparation time **10 minutes**
 plus 1 hour soaking time
Open cooking time **6 minutes**
Pressure cooking time
 10 minutes

225 g/8 oz dried black-eyed beans
1 Tbsp oil
300 g/10 oz gammon, diced
450 g/1 lb boneless, skinless
 chicken portions, diced
1 medium onion, peeled and
 chopped
1 head fennel, trimmed and diced

2 medium carrots, peeled and
 diced
One 400-g/14-oz can chopped
 tomatoes
Salt and freshly ground
 black pepper
1 tsp Cajun seasoning
2 Tbsp chopped fresh oregano
300 ml/½ pt chicken stock
350 g/12 oz sweet potatoes,
 peeled and sliced
1 Tbsp chopped fresh oregano
 or parsley

TO SERVE
Crusty bread

ASPARAGUS AND PEPPER TURKEY ROULADE

THIS DISH IS ONE OF MY ALL-TIME FAVOURITES. ALTHOUGH IT IS A LITTLE ELABORATE TO ASSEMBLE, IT IS WELL WORTH THE EFFORT.

Place the turkey steaks between 2 sheets of greaseproof paper and pound with a meat mallet until 6 mm/¼ inch thick. Place on a chopping board and set aside.

Blanch 12 to 16 asparagus spears in boiling water for 5 minutes, drain and pat dry. Place 3 to 4 asparagus spears (depending on size) and 2 to 3 strips of red pepper on each turkey steak and roll up. Wrap two slices of Parma ham round each roll and secure with fine twine.

Heat the oil in the open cooker and brown the rolls on all sides. Place the trivet rim-side down on top of the roulades and place the remaining asparagus, red pepper strips and onion wedges on top. Pour over the stock, wine, honey and soy sauce. Bring to 6.8-kg/15-lb pressure and cook for 5 minutes. Depressurize quickly and remove the roulades and vegetables from the cooker. Keep warm.

Beat the butter and flour together to form a paste. Bring the liquid in the open cooker to the boil then whisk small spoonfuls of the flour paste into the boiling liquid. Cook, stirring for 3 to 4 minutes until the sauce is thickened and glossy.

Serve, garnished with black pepper, with cooked vegetables, new potatoes and the sauce.

Serves **4**
Cook control **6.8 kg/15 lb**
Preparation time **15 minutes**
Open cooking time **8 minutes**
Pressure cooking time **5 minutes**

4 thin turkey breast steaks
350 g/12 oz baby asparagus spears, trimmed
2 red peppers, seeded and sliced
8 thin slices Parma ham
1 Tbsp oil
1 orange pepper, seeded, skinned and sliced
1 medium onion, peeled and cut into wedges
300 ml/½ pt turkey or chicken stock
150 ml/¼ pt dry white wine
2 tsp honey
2 Tbsp dark soy sauce
1 Tbsp softened butter
1 Tbsp white plain flour
Salt and freshly ground black pepper

TO GARNISH
Freshly ground black pepper

TO SERVE
Cooked vegetables and new potatoes

JAMAICAN SPICED TURKEY

IF YOUR TURKEY JOINT IS LARGER THAN 900 G/2 LB OR IS QUITE TALL IN SHAPE SO THAT THE
SEPARATOR WILL NOT SIT IN THE COOKER LEVEL, THEN COOK THE RICE SEPARATELY.

Wipe the turkey joint, make 3 to 4 slashes across the top then place in a shallow dish.
Blend the hot chilli sauce, crushed garlic, allspice, rum, ketchup and oil together.
Pour or brush over the joint, cover loosely and allow to marinate in the refrigerator
for at least 30 minutes, longer if time permits. Brush or spoon the marinade over the joint
occasionally during marinating.

Place the trivet rim-side down in the cooker and brush lightly with a little oil then pour
in the fruit juice and stock. Drain the turkey joint and place on the trivet. Close the lid
and bring to 6.8-kg/15-lb pressure. Cook for 20 minutes then depressurize quickly.

Meanwhile line the separator with foil and add the rice. Stir the chopped chilli into the rice
then pour over the hot stock. Cover with a double sheet of greaseproof paper. Place on top
of the joint and close the lid. Return to 6.8-kg/15-lb pressure and cook for 5 minutes.
Depressurize slowly and remove the rice and turkey from the cooker.

Fluff up the rice with a fork, stir in the chopped coriander and place with the turkey onto a
warmed serving dish. Garnish with coriander sprigs and mango slices.

Serves **6**
Cook control **6.8 kg/15 lb**
Preparation time **5 minutes plus**
  30 minutes marinating time
Pressure cooking time
  25 minutes

One 900-g/2-lb boneless turkey joint
2 Tbsp hot chilli sauce
4 garlic cloves, peeled and crushed
1 tsp allspice
2 Tbsp dark rum
4 Tbsp ketchup
2 Tbsp oil
250 ml/8 fl oz mango or orange juice
250 ml/8 fl oz turkey or chicken stock,
  warmed
225 g/8 oz long-grain rice
1 red jalapeño chilli
450 ml/¾ pt vegetable stock
1 Tbsp chopped fresh coriander

TO GARNISH
Coriander sprigs and mango slices

VEGETABLES

BUTTERNUT SQUASH CASSEROLE

BUTTERNUT SQUASH IS NATIVE TO TROPICAL AMERICA, BUT NOW GROWS IN EUROPE AND NORTH
AMERICA AS WELL. IT CAN BE BOILED, STEWED OR STUFFED AND BAKED.

Heat the oil in the open cooker and sauté the onion, garlic, chilli and butternut squash for 3 minutes. Add the sweet potatoes, sliced pepper and sugar, and sauté for 1 minute.

Add the chopped tomatoes with their juice, the stock or water and the Worcestershire sauce, and close the lid. Bring to 6.8-kg/15-lb pressure and cook for 3 minutes.

Depressurize quickly then add seasoning to taste and sprinkle with the chopped parsley before serving.

Serves **4**
Cook control **6.8 kg/15 lb**
Preparation time **15 minutes**
Open cooking time **4 minutes**
Pressure cooking time **3 minutes**

1 Tbsp oil
**1 medium onion, peeled and
    cut into wedges**
**3 to 5 garlic cloves, peeled
    and sliced**
1 serrano chilli, seeded and sliced
**1 small butternut squash (about
    450 g/1 lb in weight), peeled
    and diced**

**225 g/8 oz sweet potatoes, peeled
    and diced**
1 red pepper, seeded and sliced
1 green pepper, seeded and sliced
1 tsp dark brown soft sugar
**One 400-g/14-oz can chopped
    tomatoes**
**250 ml/8 fl oz vegetable stock
    or water**
1 Tbsp Worcestershire sauce
**Salt and freshly ground
    black pepper**

TO GARNISH
Chopped fresh parsley

WINTER VEGETABLE STEW

THIS IS A WARM AND HEARTY MEAL THAT IS IDEAL TO SERVE AS A MAIN COURSE
WITH WARM CRUSTY GRANARY BREAD.

Place the pearl barley in the open cooker and add 900 ml/ 1½ pints water. Close the lid and bring to 6.8-kg/15-lb pressure. Cook for 18 minutes. Depressurize slowly then remove the pearl barley from the cooker, drain and set aside. Wipe the cooker clean.

Add the oil to the open cooker and sauté the onion, garlic, parsnips, celery, carrots and potatoes for 2 minutes. Return the pearl barley to the cooker with the contents of the can of tomatoes, the stock, seasoning and chopped oregano. Close the lid and bring to 6.8-kg/15-lb pressure. Cook for 3 minutes then depressurize quickly.

Line the separator with foil and place the cabbage in the separator. Add 6 tablespoons hot water and sprinkle with the caraway seeds. Place the trivet rim-side down on top of the vegetables in the cooker and place the separator on top of the trivet. Close the lid and bring to 6.8-kg/15-lb pressure. Cook for 1 minute then depressurize quickly.

Remove the separator from the cooker and add seasoning to taste to the cabbage. Remove the trivet, adjust the seasoning and serve with the cabbage and chunks of warm granary bread.

Serves **6**
Cook control **6.8 kg/15 lb**
Preparation time **15 minutes**
Open cooking time **2 minutes**
Pressure cooking time
  22 minutes

100 g/4 oz pearl barley
1 Tbsp oil
1 large onion, peeled and cut
  into wedges
4 garlic cloves, peeled
  and chopped
2 parsnips, peeled and cut
  into wedges
3 celery sticks, trimmed
  and chopped

2 carrots, about 175 g/6 oz in
  weight, trimmed, peeled,
  and sliced
300 g/10 oz potatoes, peeled and
  cut into chunks
One 400-g/14-oz can chopped
  tomatoes
150 ml/¼ pt vegetable stock
Salt and freshly ground
  black pepper
1 Tbsp chopped fresh oregano
450 g/1 lb green cabbage,
  trimmed and shredded
1 tsp caraway seeds

TO SERVE
Warm granary bread

MAPLE-GLAZED BABY ROOT
VEGETABLES

MAPLE SYRUP IS A FAVOURITE FOR EVERYONE WITH A SWEET TOOTH, AND GOES WELL WITH PANCAKES AND DESSERTS OR, AS IN THIS RECIPE, TO FLAVOUR VEGETABLES.

Serves **4 to 6**
Cook control **6.8 kg/15 lb**
Preparation time **15 minutes**
Open cooking time **8 to 9 minutes**
Pressure cooking time **4 minutes**

8 baby onions, peeled

225 g/8 oz baby turnips, peeled

225 g/8 oz baby carrots, trimmed and peeled
  or scrubbed

225 g/8 oz baby new potatoes, scrubbed

225 g/8 oz baby parsnips, trimmed and peeled

1 Tbsp oil

1 tsp soft brown sugar

2 Tbsp maple syrup

1 tsp chilli sauce, or to taste

300 ml/½ pt vegetable stock

1 Tbsp chopped fresh thyme

Salt and freshly ground black pepper

TO GARNISH
Fresh thyme sprigs

Cut all the vegetables in halves or quarters
if necessary so they are all of a similar size.
Heat the oil in the open cooker and sauté all the
vegetables for 5 minutes. Add the sugar,
maple syrup, and chilli sauce and stir well.

Pour in the liquid then add the chopped thyme
and close the lid. Bring to 6.8-kg/15-lb pressure
and cook for 4 minutes. Depressurize quickly then
drain, reserving the liquid. Add seasoning to taste
to the vegetables, place in a serving dish,
and keep warm.

Boil the liquor in the cooker for 3 to 4 minutes
or until syrupy then pour over the vegetables
and serve garnished with the thyme sprigs.

CORN ON THE COB WITH
HERB AND GARLIC BUTTER

CORN ON THE COB IS DELICIOUS COOKED ON THE BARBECUE.
IF YOU ARE IN A HURRY, COOK THEM IN THE PRESSURE COOKER
WHILE WAITING FOR THE BARBECUE TO HEAT UP, THEN FINISH
THEM ON THE BARBECUE.

Serves **4**
Cook control **6.8 kg/15 lb**
Preparation time **5 to 8 minutes**
Pressure cooking time **10 minutes**

75 g/3 oz butter, softened

2 garlic cloves, peeled and crushed

1 Tbsp grated lemon zest

1 Tbsp chopped fresh parsley

1 Tbsp chopped fresh thyme

1 Tbsp snipped fresh chives

4 whole corn on the cob

Cream the butter until very soft then beat in the crushed garlic, lemon zest
and chopped herbs. Shape into a roll, wrap in greaseproof paper and chill in
the refrigerator for 30 minutes or until firm.

Remove and discard the outer leaves and silky threads from the corn
on the cob and rinse well.

Place in the cooker and pour in 300 ml/½ pint water. Close the lid and bring to
6.8-kg/15-lb pressure. Cook for 10 minutes then depressurize quickly.
Remove the corn on the cobs and place a large piece of herb and garlic butter
on top to serve.

FRAGRANT NEW POTATOES
WITH SHALLOTS

A PESTLE AND MORTAR IS AN INVALUABLE KITCHEN TOOL BECAUSE IT ENABLES SPICE
PODS TO BE LIGHTLY CRACKED OPEN WITHOUT LOSING THE SEEDS INSIDE THE PODS.

Heat the oil in the open cooker and sauté the lemon grass, coriander seeds, grated ginger and garlic for 2 minutes. Add the potatoes and shallots and continue to sauté for 3 minutes.

Add the coconut milk, soy sauce and stock then close the lid. Bring to 6.8-kg/15-lb pressure and cook for 4 minutes.

Depressurize quickly and drain. Discard the lemon grass stalks. Add seasoning to taste, together with the coriander, and serve.

Serves **4**
Cook control **6.8 kg/15 lb**
Preparation time **10 minutes**
Open cooking time **5 minutes**
Pressure cooking time **4 minutes**

1 Tbsp oil
2 lemon grass stalks (outer leaves discarded), lightly crushed
1 tsp coriander seeds, crushed
1 small piece root ginger, peeled and finely grated
2 garlic cloves, peeled and crushed
450 g/1 lb baby new potatoes, scrubbed
225 g/8 oz shallots, peeled
150 ml/¼ pt coconut milk
1 Tbsp light soy sauce
150 ml/¼ pt vegetable stock, heated to boiling point
Salt and freshly ground black pepper
2 Tbsp fresh coriander leaves

POTATO DAUPHINOIS

WHEN PREPARING THIS RECIPE, ENSURE THAT THE DISH YOU WISH TO USE FITS INSIDE THE PRESSURE COOKER AND THAT IT IS OVENPROOF SO YOU CAN BROWN THE CHEESE AT THE END OF COOKING UNDER THE GRILL.

Butter a round ovenproof 1.2-litre/2-pint dish. Slice the sweet potatoes fairly thickly then rinse the sweet and ordinary potatoes in cold water and pat dry with absorbent kitchen paper. Place a layer of both potatoes, the onions and garlic in the dish and pour over a little of the cream. Sprinkle with some of the grated Cheddar cheese and a little Parmesan cheese.

Repeat the layering until all the potatoes are used up, ending with a layer of cream and cheese. Cover with a double layer of greaseproof paper and secure.

Pour 600 ml/1 pint of water into the cooker and place the trivet rim-side down in the cooker. Place the dish on the trivet and close the lid. Bring to 6.8-kg/15-lb pressure and cook for 20 minutes. Depressurize quickly then remove the dish and discard the paper. Preheat the grill then cook the potatoes under the grill for 4 to 5 minutes, turning the dish occasionally until the top is golden. Serve immediately.

Serves **3 to 4**
Cook control **6.8 kg/15 lb**
Preparation time **15 minutes**
Pressure cooking time
  20 minutes

1 tsp melted butter
175 g/6 oz sweet potatoes, peeled
300 g/10 oz potatoes, peeled and
  thinly sliced
1 small onion, peeled and
  thinly sliced
2 to 4 garlic cloves, peeled
  and crushed
150 ml/¼ pint double cream
100 g/4 oz grated Cheddar cheese
2 Tbsp Parmesan cheese, grated

CREOLE OKRA STEW

WHEN USING CHILLIES REMEMBER THAT THE HEAT IS NOT ONLY IN THE SEEDS BUT ALSO IN THE MEMBRANE TO WHICH THE SEEDS ARE ATTACHED. ALWAYS WASH YOUR HANDS WELL AFTER HANDLING CHILLIES.

Serves **3 to 4**
Cook control **6.8 kg/15 lb**
Preparation time **10 minutes**
Open cooking time **5 minutes**
Pressure cooking time **2 minutes**

1 Tbsp oil
4 garlic cloves, peeled and sliced
1 to 2 green serrano chillies, seeded and chopped
1 medium onion, peeled and sliced
4 celery sticks, trimmed and chopped
1 large red pepper, seeded and chopped
100 g/4 oz green beans, trimmed and halved
225 g/8 oz okra, trimmed
1 tsp allspice
1 Tbsp chopped fresh oregano
4 medium tomatoes, (about 300 g/10 oz) chopped
150 ml/¼ pt vegetable stock, heated to boiling
Salt and freshly ground black pepper

TO GARNISH
Oregano sprigs

Heat the oil in the open cooker and sauté the garlic, chillies, onion and celery for 3 minutes. Add the red pepper, beans and okra then sprinkle in the allspice. Sauté for 2 minutes then add the oregano and tomatoes. Pour over the boiling stock.

Close the lid and bring to 6.8-kg/15-lb pressure. Cook for 3 minutes then depressurize quickly. Drain, then add seasoning to taste and serve garnished with oregano sprigs.

RED CABBAGE WITH
APPLE AND CARAWAY

COOKED RED CABBAGE TAKES ON A WONDERFULLY DEEP RICH PURPLE-RED COLOUR. COUPLED WITH ITS DELICIOUS TASTE, THIS IS ONE VEGETABLE THAT SHOULD BE PART OF ANY COOK'S REPERTOIRE.

Serves **4 to 6**
Cook control **6.8 kg/15 lb**
Preparation time **8 minutes**
Pressure cooking time
  4 minutes

1 red cabbage, about 900 g/2 lb
  in weight
1 small onion, peeled and
  thinly sliced
1 cooking apple, peeled, cored
  and sliced
2 Tbsp dark soft brown sugar
3 Tbsp cider vinegar
1 tsp caraway seeds
Salt and freshly ground
  black pepper
450 ml/¾ pt vegetable stock
  or water
1 Tbsp chopped fresh parsley

Discard any outer leaves and stalk from the cabbage and shred finely. Wash thoroughly in plenty of cold water and drain. Place in the open cooker. Add the onion, sliced apple, sugar, vinegar, caraway seeds and seasoning to taste then stir lightly. Pour over the stock and close the lid.

Bring to 6.8-kg/15-lb pressure and cook for 4 minutes. Depressurize quickly then drain off the excess liquid and serve sprinkled with the chopped parsley.

FENNEL SUPPER

FENNEL SEEMS TO BE ONE OF THOSE VEGETABLES THAT MANY PEOPLE ARE NOT QUITE SURE WHAT TO DO WITH. HERE, I HAVE COMBINED IT WITH LEEKS, CARROTS, GARLIC AND POTATOES TO CREATE A TASTY SUPPER DISH. THE GAMMON IS OPTIONAL, BUT CERTAINLY COMPLEMENTS THE FLAVOUR OF THE DISH.

Serves **4**
Cook control **6.8 kg/15 lb**
Preparation time **10 minutes**
Open cooking time **2 minutes**
Pressure cooking time
   3 minutes

1 Tbsp oil
3 garlic cloves, peeled
   and sliced
350-g/12-oz piece of gammon,
   chopped, optional
2 heads fennel, trimmed
   and sliced
2 leeks, about 300 g/10 oz,
trimmed and thickly sliced
300 g/10 oz new potatoes,
   scrubbed and thickly sliced
2 large carrots, about
   225 g/8 oz, trimmed, peeled
   and sliced
Salt and freshly ground
   black pepper
½ tsp grated fresh nutmeg
2 Tbsp chopped fresh tarragon
300 ml/½ pt vegetable stock

TO SERVE
**Freshly grated mature
   Cheddar cheese**

Heat the oil then sauté the garlic and gammon, if using, for 2 minutes. Remove the garlic and gammon and set aside.

Arrange the fennel, leeks, new potatoes and carrots in layers, sprinkling with a little of the garlic, and gammon if used. Season each layer with salt, pepper, nutmeg and a little of the chopped tarragon. When all the vegetables have been used, pour over the stock and close the lid.

Bring to 6.8 kg/15 lbs pressure and cook for 3 minutes then depressurize quickly and serve with grated cheese.

THAI VEGETABLES

BIRD'S-EYE CHILLIES ARE VERY HOT INDEED. USE SPARINGLY UNLESS YOU KNOW THAT YOU CAN TAKE THE HEAT. WEAR RUBBER GLOVES WHEN HANDLING.

Serves **4**
Cook control **6.8 kg/15 lb**
Preparation time **15 minutes**
Open cooking time **3 minutes**
Pressure cooking time
   1 minute

1 Tbsp oil
2 to 3 garlic cloves, peeled
   and crushed
2 lemon grass stalks (outer
   leaves discarded), bruised
1 small piece fresh root ginger,
   peeled and finely grated
1 to 2 bird's-eye or green
   jalapeño chillies, seeded and
   chopped
1 cinnamon stick, bruised
175 g/6 oz broccoli florets
175 g/6 oz cauliflower florets
2 carrots, peeled and chopped
1 large courgette, trimmed and
   cut into thick slices
100 g/4 oz green beans, trimmed
   and halved
150 ml/¼ pt coconut milk
Salt and freshly ground
   black pepper
fresh coriander leaves

Heat the oil in the open cooker and sauté the garlic, lemon grass, ginger, chillies and cinnamon stick for 2 minutes. Add the vegetables and sauté for 1 minute.

Pour in the coconut milk with 150 ml/¼ pt boiling water then close the lid and bring to 6.8-kg/15-lb pressure. Cook for 1 minute then depressurize quickly and discard the lemon grass and cinnamon. Season and serve sprinkled with the fresh coriander.

(For really crisp vegetables, bring to pressure then remove from the heat and depressurize quickly – for soft vegetables, pressure cook for 2 minutes.)

BROAD BEAN AND BACON SUCCOTASH

FRESH BROAD BEANS ARE ONLY IN SEASON FOR A VERY SHORT TIME SO MAKE GOOD USE OF THEM WHEN THEY ARE AVAILABLE. OTHERWISE, USE FROZEN BEANS.

Heat the oil in the open cooker and sauté the onions, garlic, chilli and gammon for 2 minutes. Add the broad beans and sweetcorn. Blend the tomato purée with the stock and pour over the vegetables.

Close the lid and bring to 6.8-kg/15-lb pressure. Cook for 2 minutes then depressurize quickly and add seasoning to taste. Drain the broad bean mixture and place in a serving bowl. Keep warm.

Bring the cooking liquid in the open cooker to the boil. Blend the cornflour with 1 tablespoon water to form a smooth paste then stir into the boiling liquid. Cook, stirring until slightly thickened and smooth. Pour over the broad bean mixture and serve sprinkled with the spring onions and the Parmesan cheese.

Serves **3 to 4**
Cook control **6.8 kg/15 lb**
Preparation time **10 minutes**
Open cooking time **5 minutes**
Pressure cooking time **2 minutes**

1 Tbsp oil
3 baby onions, peeled and cut into thin wedges
2 to 3 garlic cloves, peeled and sliced
1 jalapeño chilli, seeded and sliced
350-g/12-oz piece of gammon, derinded and chopped

350 g/12 oz broad beans, preferably fresh shelled
100 g/4 oz sweetcorn kernels
1 Tbsp tomato purée
300 ml/½ pt vegetable stock, heated to almost boiling
Salt and freshly ground black pepper
2 tsp cornflour
6 spring onions, trimmed and diagonally sliced

TO SERVE
Grated or shaved Parmesan cheese

RATATOUILLE

THIS RATATOUILLE IS SUBSTANTIAL ENOUGH TO BE SERVED AS A MAIN COURSE WITH PLENTY
OF WARM CRUSTY BREAD OR NEW POTATOES, AND PARMESAN CHEESE.

Heat the oil in the open cooker then sauté the aubergine, onion, fennel, squash, dried chillies and garlic for 3 minutes. Add the red and yellow peppers and the tomatoes and sauté for 1 minute.

Blend the tomato purée with the red wine then stir in the tomato juice and pour over the vegetables. Close the lid and bring to 6.8-kg/15-lb pressure. Cook for 2 minutes then depressurize quickly.

Remove the lid and add seasoning to taste, stir in the shredded basil and serve with shavings of Parmesan cheese.

Serves **6**
Cook control **6.8 kg/15 lb**
Preparation time **15 minutes**
Open cooking time **4 minutes**
Pressure cooking time **2 minutes**

3 Tbsp olive oil

1 aubergine, about 350 g/12 oz in weight, trimmed and diced

1 medium onion, peeled and cut into wedges

1 head fennel, trimmed and sliced

2 acorn squash, peeled, seeded and chopped

½ to 1 tsp crushed dried chillies

4 garlic cloves, peeled and chopped

1 red pepper, seeded and cut into chunks

1 yellow pepper, seeded and cut into chunks

300 g/10 oz ripe tomatoes, chopped

2 Tbsp tomato purée

150 ml/¼ pt red wine

150 ml/¼ pt tomato juice

Salt and freshly ground black pepper

2 Tbsp shredded basil

TO SERVE
Shavings of Parmesan cheese

DRIED BEANS, PASTA AND CEREALS

GREEN RICE

DIFFERENT TEXTURES ARE TO MY MIND AN INTEGRAL PART IN THE ENJOYMENT OF A MEAL. HERE THE
RAW INGREDIENTS ARE ADDED AT THE END OF THE COOKING TIME, GIVING THIS DISH ITS CRUNCH.
IF PREFERRED, HOWEVER, THEY CAN BE ADDED TO THE REST OF THE INGREDIENTS AND COOKED.

Serves **4**
Cook control **4.5 kg/10 lb**
Preparation time **5 minutes**
Pressure cooking time **2 minutes**

225 g/8 oz premixed wild and long-grain rice
1 green jalapeño chilli, seeded and chopped
2 garlic cloves, peeled and crushed
1 green pepper, seeded and chopped
100 g/4 oz fresh shelled peas
8 spring onions, trimmed and chopped
75 g/3 oz stoned pimento-stuffed olives, chopped
Salt and freshly ground black pepper
2 Tbsp chopped fresh coriander

Place the rice in the open cooker and add 1.5 litres/3 pints of water. Close the lid and bring to 4.5-kg/10-lb pressure. Cook for 2 minutes then depressurise slowly.

Add the chilli, garlic, half the green pepper and the peas. Stir well then close the lid. Return to 4.5-kg/10-lb pressure then remove from the heat and depressurise slowly.

Drain the rice thoroughly, place in a bowl and stir in the remaining chopped pepper, the spring onions, chopped olives and seasoning to taste. Mix lightly then sprinkle with the chopped coriander and serve.

BROWN RICE SALAD

THIS SALAD HAS A DISTINCT ORIENTAL FLAVOUR LOOK OUT FOR SEASONED RICE VINEGAR IN YOUR LOCAL ORIENTAL OR HEALTH FOOD STORE.

Serves **6**
Cook control **6.8 kg/15 lb**
Preparation time **12 minutes**
Open cooking time **4 minutes**
Pressure cooking time **4 minutes**

225 g/8 oz brown rice
1 tsp turmeric
Salt and freshly ground black pepper
2 Tbsp oil
2 garlic cloves, peeled and chopped
1 yellow pepper, chopped

85 g/3 oz carrot, peeled and shredded
225 g/8 oz asparagus, trimmed and cut into small pieces
8 spring onions, trimmed and chopped
4 to 6 canned water chestnuts, drained and sliced
2 Tbsp light soy sauce
3 Tbsp seasoned rice vinegar
2 Tbsp chopped fresh coriander
2 Tbsp toasted sesame seeds

Place the rice in the open cooker and add 1.5 litres/3 pints of water, tumeric, and salt to taste. Close the lid and bring to 6.8-kg/15-lb pressure. Cook for 4 minutes then depressurize slowly, drain the rice, and set aside. Wipe the cooker clean.

Heat the oil in the open cooker and sauté the garlic, pepper, carrot and asparagus for 4 minutes or until the vegetables are tender but still crisp. Return the rice to the cooker and stir in the remaining ingredients except for the sesame seeds. Stir well then turn into a serving dish, sprinkle with the sesame seeds and serve.

CHILLI BEAN POT

WHEN COOKING MORE THAN ONE TYPE OF BEAN IN THE PRESSURE COOKER MAKE SURE THEY REQUIRE THE SAME AMOUNT OF COOKING TIME.

Soak both kinds of dried beans in boiling water for 1 hour, drain and set aside.

Heat the oil in the open cooker and sauté the onion, garlic and chillies for 3 minutes. Add the tomatoes, broad beans and thyme then add the drained beans.

Blend the tomato purée with 450 ml/³/₄ pint of the stock and pour into the cooker, then bring to the boil. Close the lid and bring to 6.8-kg/15-lb pressure. Cook for 7 minutes. Depressurize slowly then stir in the mushrooms.

Line the separator with foil and place the rice into the separator. Pour over the remaining stock, cover with foil and secure.

Place the trivet rim-side down over the beans and place the rice on top. Close the lid and bring to 6.8-kg/15-lb pressure. Cook for 5 minutes. Depressurize slowly. Remove the rice from the cooker and arrange in a warm serving dish. Season the beans then spoon over the rice and garnish with the parsley.

Serves **4 to 6**
Cook control **6.8 kg/15 lb**
Preparation time **10 minutes plus**
  1 hour soaking time
Open cooking time **3 minutes**
Pressure cooking time
  12 minutes

225 g/8 oz dried red kidney beans
100 g/4 oz dried flageolet beans
1 Tbsp oil
1 medium onion, peeled and sliced
3 to 4 garlic cloves, peeled and sliced
2 to 3 serrano chillies, seeded and sliced
225 g/8 oz tomatoes, peeled and chopped
100 g/4 oz shelled broad beans
1 Tbsp chopped fresh thyme
1 Tbsp tomato purée
900 ml/1½ pt vegetable stock
100 g/4 oz closed-cup mushrooms,
  wiped and thickly chopped
225 g/8 oz long-grain rice
Salt and freshly ground black pepper

TO GARNISH
2 Tbsp chopped fresh parsley

BEAN SALAD WITH PECAN DRESSING

TO MIX THE PECANS WELL INTO THE DRESSING, PROCESS THEM WITH ALL THE HERBS IN A BLENDER
UNTIL FINELY CHOPPED OR, ALTERNATIVELY, CHOP THE BEANS AND HERBS TOGETHER BY HAND
ON A CHOPPING BOARD.

Place the beans together in a large bowl and cover with plenty of boiling water, leave for 1 hour, then drain and place in the open cooker with 900 ml/1$\frac{1}{2}$ pints cold water.

Close the lid and bring to 6.8-kg/15-lb pressure. Cook for 10 minutes, then depressurize slowly. Drain the beans and place in a large bowl.

Add the chopped spring onions, celery, shredded carrot and halved cherry tomatoes then mix lightly together.

Place the olive oil, orange juice, seasoning, garlic, orange zest, chopped herbs and pecans in a screw-top jar and shake vigorously until blended. Pour over the bean mixture and mix until the beans are lightly coated. Serve.

Serves **6 to 8**
Cook control **6.8 kg/15 lb**
Preparation time **12 minutes plus 1 hour soaking**
Pressure cooking time **10 minutes**

100 g/4 oz dried borlotti beans
100 g/4 oz dried red kidney or black-eyed beams
100 g/4 oz dried cannellini beans
8 spring onions, trimmed and chopped
3 celery sticks, trimmed and finely chopped
2 medium carrots, trimmed and shredded
175 g/6 oz cherry tomatoes, quartered
6 Tbsp olive oil
4 Tbsp orange juice
Salt and freshly ground black pepper
2 garlic cloves, peeled and crushed
1 Tbsp grated orange zest
2 Tbsp chopped fresh coriander
1 Tbsp chopped fresh flat-leaf parsley
75 g/3 oz pecans, finely chopped

WILD MUSHROOM RISOTTO

IT IS IMPORTANT WHEN USING DRIED MUSHROOMS THAT YOU REHYDRATE THEM FULLY BEFORE USE.
DO MAKE SURE THAT YOUR WATER IS NOT BOILING WHEN YOU POUR IT OVER THE MUSHROOMS
AND LEAVE FOR AT LEAST 20 MINUTES.

Place the dried mushrooms in a small bowl and cover with almost-boiling water, soak for 20 minutes, then drain, reserving the liquid and mushrooms.

Place the rice in the open cooker and add 1.5 litres/3 pints cold water. Close the lid and bring to 6.8-kg/15-lb pressure. Cook for 2 minutes then depressurize slowly, drain the rice, and reserve. Wipe the cooker clean.

Heat the oil in the open cooker then sauté the garlic, chilli and onion for 3 minutes. Add the red and yellow pepper and wild mushrooms and sauté for 1 minute. Stir in the rehydrated mushrooms and the button mushrooms with the rice. Blend the tomato purée with the reserved mushroom soaking liquid then pour into the cooker with the vegetable stock. Close the lid and bring to 6.8-kg/15-lb pressure. Depressurize slowly then add seasoning to taste and the chopped parsley, stir well and serve with the shavings of Parmesan cheese.

Serves **4**
Cook control **6.8 kg/15 lb**
Preparation time **10 minutes**
  plus 20 minutes soaking time
Open cooking time **4 minutes**
Pressure cooking time **2 minutes**

15 g/½ oz dried porcini
  mushrooms (ceps)
225 g/8 oz long-grain rice
1 Tbsp oil
6 garlic cloves, peeled and
  chopped
2 red jalapeño chillies, seeded
  and chopped
1 medium onion, peeled and
  chopped
1 red pepper, seeded
  and chopped

1 yellow pepper, seeded
  and chopped
350 g/12 oz assorted wild
  mushrooms, wiped and sliced
  if large
100 g/4 oz button mushrooms,
  wiped and sliced
2 Tbsp tomato purée
120 ml/4 fl oz vegetable stock
Salt and freshly ground black
  pepper
2 Tbsp chopped fresh flat-leaf
  parsley

TO SERVE
Shavings of Parmesan cheese

BULGHUR PILAU

IF YOU CANNOT FIND WHOLE CINNAMON STICKS, USE 1 TO 1¹/₂ TEASPOONS GROUND CINNAMON.

Heat the oil in the open cooker and sauté the garlic, onion, aubergine and cinnamon stick for 3 minutes. Add the red pepper, orange zest and half the cherry tomatoes and pour over 300 ml/¹/₂ pint of the orange juice and water. Place the trivet rim-side down on top of the vegetables.

Line the separator with foil and add the bulghur wheat. Pour in the remaining orange juice and water, cover with foil and secure. Place on the trivet.

Close the lid on the cooker and bring to 6.8-kg/15-lb pressure. Cook for 5 minutes then depressurize slowly.

Remove the separator from the cooker and place the bulghur wheat in a bowl. Stir with a fork to fluff up. Drain the vegetables then stir into the bulghur wheat with the remaining tomatoes, paprika, seasoning to taste and the almonds. Stir lightly, sprinkle with the chopped coriander and serve.

Serves **4**
Cook control **6.8 kg/15 lb**
Preparation time **15 minutes**
Open cooking time **3 minutes**
Pressure cooking time **5 minutes**

2 Tbsp olive oil
3 to 4 garlic cloves, peeled and crushed
1 medium onion, peeled and chopped
1 medium aubergine, about 350 g/12 oz in weight, trimmed and diced
1 cinnamon stick, bruised
1 red pepper, seeded and chopped
1 Tbsp grated orange zest
225 g/8 oz cherry tomatoes
600 ml/1 pt orange juice and water mixed
225 g/8 oz bulghur wheat
1 tsp paprika
Salt and freshly ground black pepper
2 Tbsp toasted flaked almonds
1 Tbsp chopped fresh coriander

PASTA WITH FRUIT AND BEANS

COOKING PASTA IN ORANGE JUICE MAY SOUND STRANGE, BUT DO TRY IT. I GUARANTEE YOU'LL LOVE IT.

Soak the dried beans in boiling water for 1 hour then drain and place in the open cooker. Add 600 ml/1 pint water and bring to the boil. Skim off any scum that floats to the surface, reduce the heat under the cooker to a gentle boil and close the lid. Bring to 6.8-kg/15-lb pressure and cook for 10 minutes. Depressurize slowly then drain the beans and set aside.

Rinse the cooker then heat the oil in the open cooker and sauté the onion, fennel and dried apricots for 2 minutes. Add the raisins, one of the apples and the orange zest, then pour over 300 ml/½ pint of the orange juice and water. Place the trivet, rim-side down, on top.

Line the separator with tin foil and add the pasta. Pour over the remaining orange juice and water.

Close the lid and bring to 6.8-kg/15-lb pressure. Cook for 2 minutes.

Depressurize slowly then strain the pasta if necessary and place in a bowl. Add the fennel and apricot mixture, the remaining diced apple, chopped spring onions, the reserved red kidney beans, seasoning to taste and the chopped coriander. Mix lightly together and serve with the grated cheese.

Serves **3 to 4**
Cook control **6.8 kg/15 lb**
Preparation time **10 minutes**
  plus 1 hour soaking time
Open cooking time **2 minutes**
Pressure cooking time **2 minutes**

175 g/6 oz dried red kidney beans
1 Tbsp olive oil
1 medium onion, peeled and
  chopped
1 head fennel, about 225 g/8 oz in
  weight, trimmed and chopped
75 g/3 oz dried apricots, chopped

50 g/2 oz raisins
2 apples, peeled, cored and diced
1 Tbsp grated orange zest
750 ml/1¼ pt orange juice and
  water mixed
175 g/6 oz dried pasta shapes
6 spring onions, trimmed and
  sliced
Salt and freshly ground black
  pepper
2 Tbsp chopped fresh coriander

TO SERVE

Grated cheese, such as Cheddar

PUY LENTIL AND RICE PILAF

PUY LENTILS VARY IN SIZE AND ARE HIGHLY REGARDED BY MANY TO BE THE BEST LENTIL.
LIKE GREEN AND CONTINENTAL LENTILS, THEY RETAIN THEIR SHAPE WHEN COOKED.

Cover the Puy lentils with boiling water, soak for 10 minutes then drain.

Heat the oil in the open cooker and sauté the garlic and onion for 3 minutes. Add the carrots and green pepper and continue to sauté for 2 minutes.

Add the drained Puy lentils with the cinnamon stick, oregano and tomatoes and stir well. Pour over 150 ml/¼ pint of the stock. Place the trivet rim-side down in the cooker.

Line the separator with foil and add the rice. Pour in the remaining stock. Cover with foil and secure. Place on the trivet and close the lid.

Bring to 6.8-kg/15-lb pressure and cook for 3 minutes. Depressurize slowly then remove the separator and fluff the rice with a fork to separate the grains.

Season the Puy lentil mixture, discard the cinnamon stick, then mix in the cooked rice and serve garnished with the oregano.

Serves **4**
Cook control **6.8 kg/15 lb**
Preparation time **10 minutes**
   plus 10 minutes soaking time
Open cooking time **5 minutes**
Pressure cooking time **3 minutes**

175 g/6 oz Puy lentils
1 Tbsp olive oil
4 garlic cloves, peeled and
   crushed
1 medium onion, peeled and
   chopped
2 medium carrots, peeled and
   cut into large chunks

1 green pepper, seeded
   and chopped
1 cinnamon stick, bruised
1 Tbsp chopped fresh oregano
4 medium tomatoes, chopped
450 ml/¾ pt vegetable stock
175 g/6 oz basmati rice
Salt and freshly ground black
   pepper

TO GARNISH
Chopped fresh oregano

SPICY PASTA

SPICES MUST BE AS FRESH AS POSSIBLE TO PROVIDE MAXIMUM FLAVOUR. IT IS BEST TO GRIND SPICES MANUALLY WITH A PESTLE AND MORTAR AS YOU NEED THEM, BUT IF THIS IS NOT POSSIBLE STORE YOUR SPICES IN A COOL DARK CUPBOARD SO THEY RETAIN AS MUCH FLAVOUR AS POSSIBLE. BUY IN SMALL QUANTITIES SO YOU USE THEM QUICKLY.

Heat the oil in the open cooker and sauté the garlic, onion, fennel and chillies for 3 minutes then sprinkle in the spices with seasoning to taste and cook for 1 minute. Add 300 ml/½ pint of the stock. Place the trivet rim-side down in the cooker.

Line the separator with foil and add the pasta, pour in the remaining stock and cover with a double sheet of greaseproof paper. Place on top of the trivet.

Close the lid and bring to 6.8-kg/15-lb pressure and cook for 2 minutes. Depressurize quickly, drain the pasta and add to the cooker with the artichoke hearts, green beans and mangetout. Close the lid and return to 6.8-kg/15-lb pressure. Depressurize slowly, adjust the seasoning, stir in the chopped coriander and serve.

Serves **4**
Cook control **6.8 kg/15 lb**
Preparation time **10 minutes**
Open cooking time **4 minutes**
Pressure cooking time **2 minutes**

1 Tbsp oil
4 garlic cloves, peeled and
   chopped
1 medium onion, peeled and
   finely sliced
1 head fennel, trimmed and
   chopped
1 to 2 green serrano chillies,
   seeded and chopped

1 tsp ground coriander
1 tsp ground cumin
1 tsp ground ginger
Salt and freshly ground black
   pepper
750 ml/1¼ pt vegetable stock
175 g/6 oz dried pasta shapes
One 400-g/14-oz can artichoke
   hearts, drained and sliced
100 g/4 oz green beans, trimmed
   and halved
100 g/4 oz mangetout, trimmed
1 Tbsp chopped fresh coriander

VEGETABLE COUSCOUS

THESE DAYS IT IS VERY EASY TO FIND INSTANT COUSCOUS. FLUFF IT UP WELL BEFORE SERVING.

Heat the oil in the open cooker and sauté the garlic, onion, sun-dried tomatoes and aubergine for 2 minutes. Add the remaining fresh vegetables and stir well. Add the chopped tomatoes and their juice with 150 ml/¼ pint of the stock, seasoning and 1 tablespoon of the chopped basil. Stir lightly. Place the trivet rim-side down on top of the vegetables.

Line the separator with foil, add the couscous and pour over the remaining stock. Cover with foil and secure. Stand on the trivet and close the lid.

Bring the cooker to 6.8-kg/15-lb pressure and cook for 3 minutes. Depressurize slowly then remove the couscous from the cooker and turn into a bowl. Add the remaining basil and softened butter and fork up until fluffy.

Arrange the vegetables on a warmed serving platter, garnish with the basil and serve with the couscous.

Serves **4**
Cook control **6.8 kg/15 lb**
Preparation time **15 minutes**
Open cooking time **2 minutes**
Pressure cooking time **3 minutes**

2 Tbsp olive oil
3 to 4 garlic cloves, peeled and crushed
1 red onion, peeled and cut into wedges
2 Tbsp sun-dried tomatoes, chopped
1 medium aubergine, trimmed and diced
1 red pepper, seeded and chopped into large pieces
1 yellow pepper, seeded and chopped into large pieces
2 medium courgettes, trimmed and diced into large chunks
One 400-g/14-oz can chopped tomatoes
300 ml/½ pt vegetable stock, almost boiling
Salt and freshly ground black pepper
2 Tbsp chopped fresh basil
225 g/8 oz couscous
3 Tbsp softened butter

TO GARNISH
Shredded basil sprigs

BROWN RICE WITH BASIL

THIS DISH MAKES A GOOD VEGETARIAN MAIN COURSE AS WELL AS AN
EXCELLENT ACCOMPANIMENT TO STEAK OR CHOPS.

Place the rice in the open cooker and add 1.5 litres/3 pints of water and salt to taste. Close the lid and bring to 6.8-kg/15-lb pressure. Cook for 4 minutes then depressurize slowly, drain the rice and set aside. Wipe the cooker clean.

Heat the oil in the open cooker and sauté the leeks, garlic and mushrooms for 2 minutes. Add the tomatoes and broccoli and pour over the stock. Close the lid, return to 6.8-kg/15-lb pressure and cook for 2 minutes. Depressurize quickly then drain off any excess stock. Spoon into a bowl and mix in the cooked rice. Blend the olive oil, lemon zest and juice together, add seasoning to taste and the basil, then pour over the rice, stir lightly and serve.

Serves **6**
Cook control **6.8 kg/15 lb**
Preparation time **15 minutes**
Open cooking time **2 minutes**
Pressure cooking time **6 minutes**

225 g/8 oz brown rice
Salt and freshly ground black
   pepper
2 Tbsp oil
2 large leeks, trimmed and sliced
4 garlic cloves, peeled and
   chopped

225 g/8 oz baby button
   mushrooms, wiped
4 medium tomatoes, seeded
   and chopped
175 g/6 oz broccoli, broken into
   small florets
300 ml/½ pt vegetable stock
3 Tbsp olive oil
1 Tbsp grated lemon zest
2 Tbsp lemon juice
2 Tbsp chopped fresh basil

HUMMUS

A MIDDLE EASTERN DISH THAT HAS PROVED TO BE VERY POPULAR IN THE WEST EITHER AS A DELICIOUS SNACKING TYPE FOOD OR AS A HEALTHY AND NUTRITIOUS STARTER.

Cover the chick peas with boiling water and soak for 1 hour. Drain and place in the cooker with 900 ml/1½ pints cold water. Bring to the boil and remove any scum from the surface with a slotted spoon. Add the garlic, lemon zest, ground cumin and chilli powder. Reduce the heat slightly then close the lid and bring to 6.8-kg/15-lb pressure. Cook for 20 minutes.

Depressurize slowly then drain the chick peas and place in a food processor. Add the lemon juice and tahini paste and blend to a coarse purée. With the motor still running, slowly pour in sufficient olive oil to give a smooth purée. Add seasoning to taste.

Scrape into a small serving bowl, sprinkle with the toasted pine kernels and paprika and serve with strips of warm pitta bread.

Serves **8**
Cook control **6.8 kg/15 lb**
Preparation time **10 minutes plus**
  1 hour soaking time
Pressure cooking time
  20 minutes

225 g/8 oz chick peas
4 to 6 garlic cloves, peeled
1 to 1½ Tbsp grated lemon zest
1 tsp ground cumin
1 tsp mild chilli powder
3 Tbsp lemon juice
2 to 3 Tbsp tahini paste
About 300 ml/½ pt olive oil
Salt and freshly ground black pepper

TO GARNISH
2 Tbsp toasted pine kernels and paprika

TO SERVE
Strips of warm pitta bread

DESSERTS
AND PRESERVES

CHOCOLATE STEAMED PUDDINGS

THIS IS AN ELEGANT DESSERT TO SERVE AT A DINNER PARTY.

Lightly oil and line the bases of four individual pudding bowls or ramekins. (Ensure they will all fit into the cooker.) Stir the chocolate to ensure there are no lumps and allow to cool.

Cream the butter and sugar together then gradually beat in the eggs, adding a little flour after each addition. When all the eggs have been added, stir in the melted chocolate and then the remaining flour. Stir well then divide among the four bowls and level the top. Cover each with a double sheet of greaseproof paper or oiled sheet of foil with a pleat in the centre and secure firmly with twine.

Place the trivet rim-side down in the cooker and pour 900 ml/1$\frac{1}{2}$ pints boiling water and a little lemon juice into the cooker. Place the puddings on the trivet. Close the lid and presteam for 5 minutes.

Bring the cooker to 6.8-kg/15-lb pressure and cook for 7 minutes then release the steam slowly for about 10 minutes. Turn out and serve dusted with icing sugar, berries and a sauce of your choice. (If using foil add an extra 3 minutes to the cooking time.)

Serves **4**
Cook control **6.8 kg/15 lb**
Preparation time **10 to 15 minutes**
Presteaming time **5 minutes**
Pressure cooking time **7 minutes**

50 g/2 oz plain dark chocolate, melted
100 g/4 oz unsalted butter
100 g/4 oz light soft brown sugar
2 small eggs, beaten
100 g/4 oz self-raising flour

TO SERVE
Icing sugar, fresh summer berries and chocolate or red fruit sauce

STICKY TOFFEE PUDDING

THIS STICKY TOFFEE PUDDING IS A PERFECT, COMFORTING DESSERT TO SERVE ON A COLD DAY.

Oil a 900-ml/1½-pint pudding basin and place a small circle of oiled greaseproof paper in the base. Set aside.

Cream the butter and sugar together then gradually beat in the eggs with a little of the flour. When all the eggs have been added, stir in the golden syrup followed by the remaining flour, the dates and the pecans.

Turn into the prepared basin, ensuring that the bowl is only filled two-thirds full. Cover with a double sheet of greaseproof paper and secure firmly with fine twine.

Place the trivet rim-side down in the cooker and stand the bowl on top of the trivet.

Pour in 900 ml/1½ pints boiling water with a little lemon juice. Close the lid and presteam for 15 minutes. Bring to 4.5-kg/10-lb pressure and cook for 25 to 30 minutes.

Depressurize slowly then remove the lid, carefully remove the pudding and turn out onto a serving plate.

Meanwhile make the sauce by melting the butter, sugar and golden syrup together, stirring frequently. Once the sugar has dissolved, slowly stir in the cream, bring to the boil and boil gently for 2 minutes. Serve with the pudding and extra pecans if liked.

Serves **6**
Cook control **4.5 kg/10 lb**
Preparation time **10 minutes**
Presteaming time **15 minutes**
Pressure cooking time
  25 to 30 minutes

FOR THE SPONGE
2 tsp oil
100 g/4 oz unsalted butter
100 g/4 oz dark soft brown sugar

2 medium eggs, beaten
100 g/4 oz self-raising flour
2 Tbsp golden syrup
100 g/4 oz chopped stoned dates
50 g/2 oz pecans, chopped

FOR THE SAUCE
50 g/2 oz unsalted butter
50 g/2 oz dark soft brown sugar
2 Tbsp golden syrup
250 ml/8 fl oz single cream

ORANGE AND APRICOT
CRÈME BRÛLÉE

IF LIKED YOU CAN VARY THE DRIED FRUIT. TRY DRIED CRANBERRIES OR BLUEBERRIES OR A MIXTURE OF BOTH. FRESH FRUITS CAN ALSO BE USED BUT THESE NEED TO BE FIRM IN TEXTURE SO THAT THEY DO NOT BREAK UP DURING COOKING.

Lightly oil four 150-ml/¼-pint ramekin dishes, place the chopped apricots in the bases and set aside. Heat the cream with the orange zest and orange-flower water to just below boiling point then remove from the heat and reserve.

Whisk the egg yolks with the caster sugar until creamy then whisk in the cream mixture. Pour over the apricots and cover each dish with a double sheet of greaseproof paper and secure.

Place the trivet rim-side down into the cooker and pour 300 ml/1½ pints boiling water and the lemon juice into the cooker. Place the ramekins onto the trivet, close the lid and bring to 6.8-kg/15-lb pressure. Cook for 4 minutes then depressurize slowly.

Carefully remove and discard the greaseproof paper then chill for at least 4 hours.

Sprinkle the tops with the demerara sugar then place under a preheated grill and cook, turning the ramekins frequently until the sugar dissolves and caramelises. Chill again before serving. Garnish with mint sprigs and apricots.

(You may find that four ramekins do not fit inside the cooker. If so, either do in two batches or use mini ramekins.)

Serves **4**
Cook control **6.8 kg/15 lb**
Preparation time **5 minutes plus chilling time**
Open cooking time **4 minutes**
Pressure cooking time **4 minutes**

75 g/3 oz dried apricots, chopped
600 ml/1 pt whipping cream
1 Tbsp finely grated orange zest
1 Tbsp orange-flower water
4 large egg yolks
1 Tbsp caster sugar
1 Tbsp lemon juice
50 g/2 oz demerara sugar

TO GARNISH
Mint sprigs and fresh sliced apricots or extra dried apricots

WHITE BURGUNDY PEARS

CHOOSE FIRM PEARS OF A SIMILAR SIZE AND SHAPE THAT WILL FIT COMFORTABLY INTO THE PRESSURE COOKER.
TRY THEM WITH DIFFERENT FLAVOURS OF ICE CREAM AS AN ACCOMPANIMENT.

Serves **6**
Cook control **6.8 kg/15 lb**
Preparation time **5 minutes**
Open cooking time **3 minutes**
Pressure cooking time **3 minutes**

6 dessert pears
1 small orange
300 ml/½ pt white burgundy wine
6 cloves
2 cinnamon sticks, bruised
50 g/2 oz sugar
2 Tbsp brandy

TO GARNISH
Mint sprigs and extra pared orange zest

TO SERVE
Sweet biscuits and vanilla ice cream

Peel the pears as thinly as possible, keeping the stalks intact. Set aside. Pare the zest from the orange and squeeze out the juice.

Place the pears in the cooker with the orange zest, juice, wine, cloves, cinnamon and sugar. Spoon the wine a few times over the pears then close the lid. Bring to 6.8-kg/15-lb pressure and cook for 3 minutes.

Depressurize slowly then remove the lid and lift out the pears. Set aside on a serving dish.

Add the brandy to the liquid in the cooker, bring to a rapid boil and boil for 3 minutes. Strain over the pears, then cool and chill until required.

Decorate with mint sprigs and pared orange zest and serve with biscuits and ice cream.

LEMON DRIZZLE PUDDING

WHEN DONE, THIS PUDDING SEPARATES INTO TWO, GIVING A DELICIOUS LEMONY SAUCE ON THE BASE TOPPED WITH A LIGHT FLUFFY SPONGE.

Serves **6**
Cook control **4.5 kg/10 lb**
Preparation time **12 minutes**
Presteaming time **15 minutes**
Pressure cooking time
10 minutes

100 g/4 oz unsalted butter, softened
200 g/7 oz caster sugar
2 medium eggs, beaten
75 g/3 oz self-raising flour
2 Tbsp finely grated lemon zest
2 Tbsp ground almonds
½ tsp baking powder, sieved
4 Tbsp lemon juice
1 Tbsp icing sugar

Lightly oil a 1.5-litre/2½-pint ovenproof dish. Cream the butter with 100 g/4 oz of the caster sugar until light and fluffy then gradually beat in the eggs a little at a time, adding 2 teaspoons of flour with each addition.

When all the eggs have been added, stir in 1 tablespoon of lemon zest with the remaining flour, the ground almonds and baking powder. Spoon into the prepared dish.

Mix the remaining sugar, lemon zest and juice with 300 ml/½ pint of boiling water and pour into the dish. Cover with a double layer of greaseproof paper with a pleat in the centre and secure.

Place the trivet rim-side down in the cooker with an extra 2 tablespoons of lemon juice. Place the dish into the cooker and pour in 900 ml/1½ pints boiling water.

Close the lid and presteam for 15 minutes. Bring to 4.5-kg/10-lb pressure and cook for 10 minutes. Depressurize slowly and serve sprinkled with the sieved icing sugar.

DRIED FRUIT COMPOTE

CHOOSE YOUR FAVOURITE DRIED FRUIT AND SERVE
WITH PLENTY OF CREAM OR CRÈME FRAÎCHE.

Serves **4 to 6**
Cook control **6.8 kg/15 lb**
Preparation time **3 minutes**
   plus 10 minutes soaking time
Pressure cooking time
   10 minutes

225 g/8 oz dried fruit salad
225 g/8 oz dried figs or apricots
4 to 5 cardamom pods, bruised
50 g/2 oz light soft brown sugar
2 Tbsp brandy

TO SERVE
Lightly whipped cream or crème
   fraîche and sweet biscuits

Place the dried fruits in a large bowl, cover with 900 ml/ 1¹/₂ pints
boiling water and leave for 10 minutes.

Drain, reserving the soaking liquid, and arrange in layers with
the cardamom pods and sugar in the cooker, then pour over the
soaking liquid and the brandy. Close the lid and bring to 6.8-kg/
15-lb pressure. Cook for 10 minutes then depressurize slowly.

Remove from the cooker and serve warm or chilled with the
cream or crème fraîche and biscuits.

BARBECUE RELISH

THIS DELICIOUS RELISH IS IDEAL TO SERVE WITH
MOST MEATS, AND ALSO GOES WELL WITH CHEESE.

Makes **1.5 kg/3 lb**
Cook control **4.5 kg/10 lb**
Preparation time **15 minutes**
Open cooking time **20 minutes**
Pressure cooking time
   10 minutes

675 g/1½ lb cooking apples,
   peeled, cored and chopped
900 g/2 lb ripe but firm
   tomatoes, chopped

1 large onion, peeled and
   chopped
4 garlic cloves, peeled and
   crushed
2 to 3 red chillies, seeded and
   chopped
2 tsp whole-grain mustard
2 Tbsp tomato purée
450 ml/¾ pt red wine vinegar
225 g/8 oz dark soft brown sugar
2 Tbsp chopped fresh coriander

Place the cooking apples, tomatoes, onion, garlic and chillies
into the open cooker then stir in the mustard, tomato purée,
and 300 ml/¹/₂ pint vinegar. Stir well then close the lid and bring
to 4.5-kg/10-lb pressure. Cook for 10 minutes.

Depressurize slowly then stir in the remaining vinegar, the sugar
and chopped coriander. Place over a gentle heat and stir until the
sugar has dissolved.

Increase the heat and boil for about 20 minutes or until a thick
consistency is reached. Pot into sterilised warm jars and cover
with greaseproof discs. Once cold, cover, label and store in a cool
dark place and use within 3 months.

LEMON CURD

FEW THINGS ARE MORE DELICIOUS THAN HOME-MADE LEMON CURD SPREAD ON FRESHLY BAKED BREAD.

Beat the eggs and strain into a bowl that fits easily inside the cooker. Stir in the sugar, lemon zest and juice. Cut the butter into small pieces and add to the bowl then cover with a double thickness of greaseproof paper. Secure firmly around the rim with twine.

Pour 450 ml/¾ pint water and a little lemon juice into the cooker with the trivet rim-side down. Put the bowl into the cooker and close the lid.

Bring to 6.8-kg/15-lb pressure and cook for 10 minutes. Release the steam slowly. Carefully remove the greaseproof paper, whisk the lemon curd well (it may have separated a little) until thick and smooth then put into a sterilised warm jar. Cover with a tightly fitting lid and store in the refrigerator for up to one week.

Makes **one 450-g/1-lb jar**
Cook control **6.8 kg/15 lb**
Preparation time **12 to 15 minutes**
Pressure cooking time **10 minutes**

3 medium eggs
225 g/8 oz caster sugar
Finely grated zest of 2 lemons,
    preferably unwaxed
3 Tbsp lemon juice
50 g/2 oz unsalted butter

APRICOT CHUTNEY

THIS RECIPE ENABLES YOU NOT ONLY TO USE YOUR OWN HOME-GROWN FRUIT AND VEGETABLES
BUT ALSO TO EXPERIMENT WITH DIFFERENT FLAVOURS.

Makes **Four 450-g/1-lb jars**
Cook control **6.8 kg/15 lb**
Preparation time **10 minutes plus 10 minutes**
  soaking time
Open cooking time **5 to 10 minutes**
Pressure cooking time **10 minutes**

450 g/1 lb dried apricots
450 g/1 lb cooking apples, peeled, cored and chopped
225 g/8 oz raisins
1 large onion, peeled and chopped
2 to 3 red chillies, seeded and chopped
2 Tbsp ground ginger
Grated zest and juice of 1 lemon
450 ml/¾ pint white wine vinegar
225 g/8 oz light soft brown sugar

Place the apricots in a bowl, cover with boiling water and soak for 10 minutes. Drain and chop then place in the cooker with the apple, raisins, onion, chillies, ginger, lemon zest and juice, and 300 ml/½ pint of the vinegar.

Stir well, close the lid, bring to 6.8-kg/15-lb pressure and cook for 10 minutes before releasing the pressure slowly.

Stir in the remaining vinegar and sugar. Boil in the open cooker stirring occasionally for 5 to 10 minutes or until a thick consistency is formed. Put in warm sterilised jars and cover tightly. Store in the refrigerator up to 3 weeks.

MIXED CITRUS MARMALADE

SEVILLE ORANGES ARE WONDERFUL FOR MAKING MARMALADE, BUT THEY HAVE A VERY SHORT SEASON. WHEN THEY ARE UNAVAILABLE, I MAKE THIS MARMALADE, WHICH IS QUITE EASY TO PREPARE AND TASTES DELICIOUS.

Makes **Seven 450-g/1-lb jars**
Cook control **6.8 kg/15 lb**
Preparation time **35 minutes**
Open cooking time **15 minutes**
Pressure cooking time
  10 minutes

2 large oranges
1 red grapefruit
2 lemons
1.75 kg/4 lb
preserving sugar
1 Tbsp butter

Scrub the fruit, halve it and squeeze out the juice. Cut the fruit into quarters. Remove the pips and pith from the fruit and place them in a piece of muslin or cheesecloth, then tie to secure.

Place all the fruit juice, the fruit quarters, the muslin bag and 600 ml/ 1 pint water into the cooker and close the lid. Bring to 6.8-kg/15-lb pressure and cook for 10 minutes then depressurize quickly.

Remove and discard the muslin bag with the pith and pips. Strain the juice, then return to the cooker. When the fruit quarters are cool enough to handle, shred into thick strips then return to the cooker.

Add the sugar and a further 300 ml/½ pint water then return to the heat and cook, stirring frequently until the sugar has dissolved.

Add the butter then bring to the boil and boil rapidly until setting point is reached. Skim if necessary then pot into warm sterilised jars and cover tightly. Store in the refrigerator up to 1 month.

INDEX